EXAMINING THE EFFECTIVENESS OF THE KINGPIN DESIGNATION ACT IN THE WESTERN HEMISPHERE

HEARING

BEFORE THE

SUBCOMMITTEE ON
THE WESTERN HEMISPHERE

OF THE

COMMITTEE ON FOREIGN AFFAIRS
HOUSE OF REPRESENTATIVES

ONE HUNDRED FIFTEENTH CONGRESS

FIRST SESSION

NOVEMBER 8, 2017

Serial No. 115–86

Printed for the use of the Committee on Foreign Affairs

Available via the World Wide Web: http://www.foreignaffairs.house.gov/ or
http://www.gpo.gov/fdsys/

U.S. GOVERNMENT PUBLISHING OFFICE

27–514PDF   WASHINGTON : 2017

For sale by the Superintendent of Documents, U.S. Government Publishing Office
Internet: bookstore.gpo.gov   Phone: toll free (866) 512–1800; DC area (202) 512–1800
Fax: (202) 512–2104   Mail: Stop IDCC, Washington, DC 20402–0001

COMMITTEE ON FOREIGN AFFAIRS

EDWARD R. ROYCE, California, *Chairman*

CHRISTOPHER H. SMITH, New Jersey
ILEANA ROS-LEHTINEN, Florida
DANA ROHRABACHER, California
STEVE CHABOT, Ohio
JOE WILSON, South Carolina
MICHAEL T. McCAUL, Texas
TED POE, Texas
DARRELL E. ISSA, California
TOM MARINO, Pennsylvania
MO BROOKS, Alabama PAUL
COOK, California SCOTT
PERRY, Pennsylvania RON
DeSANTIS, Florida
MARK MEADOWS, North Carolina
TED S. YOHO, Florida
ADAM KINZINGER, Illinois
LEE M. ZELDIN, New York
DANIEL M. DONOVAN, JR., New York
F. JAMES SENSENBRENNER, JR.,
  Wisconsin
ANN WAGNER, Missouri
BRIAN J. MAST, Florida
FRANCIS ROONEY, Florida
BRIAN K. FITZPATRICK, Pennsylvania
THOMAS A. GARRETT, JR., Virginia
VACANT

ELIOT L. ENGEL, New York
BRAD SHERMAN, California
GREGORY W. MEEKS, New York
ALBIO SIRES, New Jersey
GERALD E. CONNOLLY, Virginia
THEODORE E. DEUTCH, Florida
KAREN BASS, California
WILLIAM R. KEATING, Massachusetts
DAVID N. CICILLINE, Rhode Island
AMI BERA, California
LOIS FRANKEL, Florida
TULSI GABBARD, Hawaii
JOAQUIN CASTRO, Texas
ROBIN L. KELLY, Illinois
BRENDAN F. BOYLE, Pennsylvania
DINA TITUS, Nevada
NORMA J. TORRES, California
BRADLEY SCOTT SCHNEIDER, Illinois
THOMAS R. SUOZZI, New York
ADRIANO ESPAILLAT, New York
TED LIEU, California

AMY PORTER, *Chief of Staff*   THOMAS SHEEHY, *Staff Director*
JASON STEINBAUM, *Democratic Staff Director*

———

SUBCOMMITTEE ON THE WESTERN HEMISPHERE

PAUL COOK, CALIFORNIA, *Chairman*

CHRISTOPHER H. SMITH, New Jersey
ILEANA ROS-LEHTINEN, Florida
MICHAEL T. McCAUL, Texas
MO BROOKS, Alabama
RON DeSANTIS, Florida
TED S. YOHO, Florida
FRANCIS ROONEY, Florida

ALBIO SIRES, New Jersey
JOAQUIN CASTRO, Texas
ROBIN L. KELLY, Illinois
NORMA J. TORRES, California
ADRIANO ESPAILLAT, New York
GREGORY W. MEEKS, New York

C O N T E N T S

Page

WITNESSES

LETTERS, STATEMENTS, ETC., SUBMITTED FOR THE HEARING

APPENDIX

EXAMINING THE EFFECTIVENESS OF THE KINGPIN DESIGNATION ACT IN THE WESTERN HEMISPHERE

WEDNESDAY, NOVEMBER 8, 2017

House of Representatives,
Subcommittee on the Western Hemisphere,
Committee on Foreign Affairs,
Washington, DC.

The subcommittee met, pursuant to notice, at 2:00 p.m., in room 2172, Rayburn House Office Building, Hon. Paul Cook (chairman of the subcommittee) presiding.

Mr. COOK. A quorum being present, the subcommittee will come to order. Without objection, all members will have 5 days to submit statements, questions, and extraneous materials for the record, subject to the length limitations for the rules.

I would like to recognize myself for 5 minutes for my opening statement.

Today's hearing marks the beginning of my time as chair of the Western Hemisphere Subcommittee leadership. I am honored to assume the chairmanship and continue the good works of the subcommittee and the full committee chairman, Ed Royce, in promoting American interests in the Western Hemisphere.

This subcommittee has a long history of bipartisanship, and I look forward to continuing that tradition with my ranking member and other subcommittee members.

The United States has significant security, economic, and political interests in the Arctic, Canada, Central America, and the Caribbean and South America. And I am deeply supportive of greater U.S. engagement with our partners and friends in these places.

As U.S. Southern Command Admiral Tidd testified to Congress in April, Latin American and the Caribbean is the region most connected to our own society, prosperity, and security, and we are linked by our shared values, cultures, and the rapid flow of goods, services, people and information throughout our hemisphere. To that end, today's subcommittee hearing is significant with an increasing number of transnational criminal networks exploiting those links for the purposes of drug trafficking and other illicit activities.

In fact, according to the U.N. Office on Drugs and Crime, revenue from illegal drugs may account for 50 percent of all transnational organized crime proceeds. These developments have a direct impact on the United States where we are struggling with an opioid crisis that claimed more than 59,000 American lives last year and results in 91 Americans lost every day according to the Center for Disease Control.

Last year's White House national drug control strategy noted significant increases in the number of Americans using cocaine, heroin, marijuana, and methamphetamine. Many of these illicit drugs are produced in foreign countries in the Western Hemisphere and are sent here to feed American demand. Illicit drugs have caused American deaths and contributed to horrible violence in our neighbors as criminal groups vie for power and control of trafficking routes.

Moreover, 6 of the 10 top countries with the highest murder rates in the world this year are in the Western Hemisphere. It is imperative that we work proactively with our regional partners to fight back against the crime and violence plaguing our nations. It is against this backdrop that we meet today to conduct oversight of a key tool the United States has used since 1999 to target drug traffickers and their supporters—the Foreign Narcotics Kingpin Designation Act, or Kingpin Act. The Kingpin Act builds on Executive Order 12978, issued in 1995, which was focused solely on Colombia and was the first ever U.S. economic sanctions program administered by the Treasury Department's Office of Foreign Assets Control to address drug trafficking.

In brief, the Kingpin Act blocks all property and assets of designated entities and those who support them. It prohibits U.S. transactions with designated entities. It establishes an annual process for sanctioning the most significant foreign narcotics traffickers. It increases civil and criminal penalties, and it prevents drug traffickers' spouses and children from getting visas to the United States.

In 2011 President Obama issued Executive Order 13581 establishing another sanctions program targeting transnational criminal networks that threaten U.S. national security, foreign policy, or economic interests. In February, President Trump signed executive order 13773 prioritizing Federal law enforcement responses to transnational organized crime. The State Department's Bureau of International Narcotics and Law Enforcement Affairs also publishes an annual report to Congress providing the factual basis for designations on major drug transit and major illicit drug-producing countries. The State Department designates countries that are vulnerable to money laundering by drug traffickers and one-third of the countries of the primary concern are in the Western Hemisphere.

These rules appear useful to U.S. objectives to counter drug flows and transnational criminal networks. However, Congress has an interest in ensuring these tools are coordinating with lasting results.

The Kingpin Act has been around for a long time and has led to hundreds of individuals and entities being sanctioned. As of October, of the 110 top-tier kingpin designations, 65 individuals and 16 organizations are connected to countries in the Western Hemisphere. Over the years, the Kingpin Act has expanded, and it is now utilized globally.

A lot of changing dynamics in terms of the drug cartels and different things in the global use of the Kingpin Act necessitate a review to consider lessons learned in the Western Hemisphere. It is important to note that while the FARC and Urabenos in Colombia are both designated as kingpins, the National Liberation Front, the ELN, is not. Similarly, although MS-13 is designated under the transnational crimes sections program, it is not sanctioned as a kingpin.

Hezbollah, although listed as a foreign terrorist organization, is not sanctioned as a kingpin in any country in the Western Hemisphere. What are we losing by not including these groups in further sanctions, especially given the dangerous nexus between multinational drug operations and terror operations?

The Kingpin Act was recently used against the Venezuelan Government officials and Mexican drug cartel operatives. How are we measuring these objectives since its inception? Has the act lead to fewer arrests coming into the United States?

I look forward to hearing from our experts, and I will now yield to the ranking member on the subcommittee for his opening statement.

Mr. SIRES. Well, good afternoon, and thank you for being here.

I would like to start by welcoming our new chairman, Mr. Cook. I look forward to working with you. We are happy to have you here leading the subcommittee, and I look forward to a good relationship.

Today's hearing focuses on the Kingpin Designation Act, a powerful tool the U.S. has used against drug traffickers and money launderers around the world since President Clinton's administration. The Kingpin Act allows the U.S. Government to target narcotic traffickers and senior members of their organizations. Dismantling these powerful organizations by going after their financial network instead of arresting low-level criminals in the streets can help take apart an organization permanently instead of trying to put a Band-Aid on an open wound.

These designations have been used all over the world to target powerful drug traffickers and have helped bring down criminals who were previously thought to be untouchable. Going after groups like the Cali cartel in Colombia showed the world that no amount of money could protect the criminal network.

Today, the Kingpin Act has targeted criminals all over the world, reaching from Mexico, Honduras, Colombia, to India, Afghanistan, and Lebanon. However, the process to designate an individual or an entity under the Kingpin Act can be long and murky. There are questions about how decisions are made and how the interagency process is used to coordinate these designations that frequently relate to politically sensitive foreign policies. We also need to look closely at whether these agencies have the resources they need to thoroughly investigate the targets in a timely manner.

Most importantly, we must remember the kingpin designation act and all the sanctions are a tool, not an end goal. Without a clear focus of policy toward a country or criminal organization, these designations will do nothing more than stir up a few press releases and create uncertainty in already unstable countries.

I am eager to listen to our witnesses today to learn how the designation process may be strengthened so that we can effectively combat criminal organizations around the world and especially here in the Western Hemisphere.

Thank you, and I yield back the balance of my time.

Mr. COOK. Thank you, Mr. Sires.

Before I recognize our witnesses, I was going to—normally, I would like to have opening statements. But if they will indulge me, because we have got four witnesses here, and I have a lot of questions. And I would rather err on the side of questions so that we can get right to the point.

And before I provide you your testimony, I am going to explain the lighting system in front of you. Very complicated. You are going to have 5 minutes. Try to stick to that. I will try to be polite, and then, you know, you go on, and on, and on like some Members of Congress, I will break the gavel. But when you begin, the light will turn green. When you have a minute left, it will turn yellow. When your time has expired, the light will turn red. And then, as I said, I don't mean for you to just to stop in mid-sentence. But you get the cue. It depends. If it is good stuff, yes.

After our witnesses testify, members will have 5 minutes to ask questions. I urge my colleagues to stick to the 5-minute rule. We don't have many here today, but I hope others will be watching us on TV. What an important hearing this is, and they are all going to descend here and all the seats are going to be filled.

Today we are going to be hearing from four witnesses. First let me introduce Mr. Donald C. Semesky, Jr. Mr. Semesky spent 44 years in the U.S. Federal law enforcement, 30 years with the U.S. Internal Review Service, criminal investigation, and 14 with the United States Drug Enforcement Agency, 5 years as the Chief of the Office of Financial Operations, and 9 years as a money laundering subject matter expert consultant. I think that adds up to about 156 years. God, whatever you are taking, I want some of it. Mr. Semesky, thank you for joining us today.

And I am going to introduce each panel member as we go along. So right now, unless you have any objections, you will be recognized for 5 minutes.

STATEMENT OF MR. DONALD C. SEMESKY JR. (FORMER CHIEF, OFFICE OF FINANCIAL OPERATIONS, U.S. DRUG ENFORCEMENT ADMINISTRATION)

Mr. SEMESKY. Thank you, Mr. Chairman.

Chairman Cook, Ranking Member Sires, and distinguished members of the House of Representatives Subcommittee on the Western Hemisphere, first, thank you, very much, for allowing me to appear before you today to discuss the effectiveness of the Kingpin Act.

I believe that my written statement and my testimony, as well as my answers today, will help you understand more of the tremendously effective impact that this has had on protecting the United States from the scourge of illegal drugs and the flow of money back to these organizations.

One of the things I want my testimony to really hone in on is the use of the Kingpin Act as an effective law enforcement tool, not just a sanctions tool. You know, where we have been able to work very closely with the Office of Foreign Assets Control, Department of Treasury, as part of our investigative process, to target and take down, simultaneously with the sanctions, major foreign drug operations and money laundering operations.

I will preface my remarks by saying that I am not here as a representative of the Drug Enforcement Administration today. I am here as a private citizen, although I did spend, as Congressman Cook highlighted, 5 years as the Chief of Financial Operations. During that tenure, I worked very closely with the Office of Foreign Assets Control and helped bring them into DEA headquarters, open up DEA data to them, and then stand up a memorandum of understanding and the standard operating procedure by which that office, which is commonly referred to as OFAC, uses drug enforcement administration information in their targeting and designation process.

My written statement outlines the designation process, so I will not go through that except to say that OFAC works very closely with the interagency law enforcement partners, with the Department of Defense, and with the intelligence community in targeting and vetting their designees prior to the actual designation.

As I mentioned, OFAC and DEA operate under a memorandum of understanding and standard operating procedure in accessing DEA's information and then vetting it through our agency before they can use it in their investigative reports. OFAC has a permanently assigned investigator to DEA headquarters and also another one permanently assigned to our special operations division in Virginia.

As you know, I am sure, the agency also has permanently assigned investigators in both the Embassy in Bogota, Colombia, and the U.S. Embassy in Mexico city, Mexico. This allows for on-the-ground investigation by those members of OFAC into foreign drug kingpins, foreign drug money laundering organizations, and it also allows the Ambassadors in those countries to get in-depth briefings on pending actions so they can make the decisions they have to on the political and financial ramifications that it is going to have on their area of operation.

I have personally witnessed at many different levels in these countries the business community and the financial community's interest in the Kingpin Act and their interest in dealing with, on a day-to-day basis, the representatives of OFAC in those Embassies. They are always the most sought after people in the Embassy for those sectors, and they are at every conference, financial conference, business conference, throughout Latin America. So that alone speaks to the impact of the agency.

My statement talks about two examples of the effectiveness. One is, as you mentioned, Cali, Colombia the Rodriguez Orejuela brothers waived extradition and turned themselves over to U.S. authorities for the sole purpose of removing their families from the OFAC designation list. The other investigation is the recently concluded Rosenthal family enterprise in Honduras which laundered drug money throughout Latin America, and that enterprise has been completely dismantled because of a joint law enforcement and sanctions activity.

I will conclude with one final recommendation. And that would be that the Kingpin Act has never been included as a specified unlawful activity in the Federal money laundering statute. And it would be very helpful if that violation could be included so when drug kingpins that cannot be touched for any other reason conduct financial transactions, we can bring charges using that as the violation.

Thank you, Mr. Chairman.

[The prepared statement of Mr. Semesky follows:]

House Committee on Foreign Affairs

Subcommittee on the Western Hemisphere

"Examining the Effectiveness of the Kingpin Designation Act in the Western Hemisphere"

Written Statement of Mr. Donald C. Semesky, Jr., Former Chief, U.S. Drug Enforcement Administration, Office of Financial Operations (Retired)

November 8, 2017

Introduction

Chairman Cook, Ranking Member Sires, and distinguished members of the House of Representatives, Subcommittee on the Western Hemisphere, thank you for allowing me to appear before you today to discuss the effectiveness of the Kingpin Act. I believe this law has had been tremendously effective in protecting the United States from the scourge of illegal drugs by allowing Federal law enforcement authorities to impact foreign Kingpin drug traffickers and money launderers, many times in situations where these criminals have insulated themselves from traditional law enforcement processes.

I must preface my remarks today by stating that I am appearing as a citizen, and not as a representative of the Drug Enforcement Administration (DEA), and my testimony should not be construed as the position of the agency. I am a retired Chief of Financial Operations with the DEA; and, during my tenure in that position, and since as a consultant to DEA, have had the opportunity to work very closely with the Office of Foreign Assets Control (OFAC), to include serving on the OFAC Kingpin Committee. I have also witnessed how this sanctions authority has grown into one of the most effective enforcement tools that the Drug Enforcement Administration has at its disposal in dealing with international sources of drug supply.

Background

On October 21, 1995 President Clinton signed Executive Order 12978, entitled Blocking Assets and Prohibiting Transactions With Significant Narcotics Traffickers. This list specifically targeted the Cali (Drug) Cartel, but was eventually expanded to include all Colombian-based cartel leaders. Under this Executive Order these designees were called "Specially Designated Narcotics Traffickers (SDNT). This list became known, and is still known in Colombia as *La Lista Clinton,* i.e. The Clinton List.

Based on the success of the SDNT Program, Congress passed The Foreign Narcotics Kingpin Designation Act, also known as the Kingpin Act, as part of the Intelligence Authorization Act for Fiscal Year 2000. The Kingpin Act was signed into law by President Clinton on December 3, 1999.

Since 2010, all OFAC designations of narcotics traffickers and drug money launderers have been done under the authority of the Kingpin Act. As part of this enforcement effort, OFAC publishes a list of individuals and companies owned or controlled by, or acting for or on behalf of, targeted individuals and organizations. The assets of these designated individuals, organizations and legal entities that are within the jurisdiction of the United States are blocked; and, U.S. persons are generally prohibited from dealing with them.

OFAC has two sides within its infrastructure, an investigative/enforcement side that investigates and puts together the reports justifying the designation, and a compliance side that works with the financial services industry, individuals and businesses within the U.S. and around the world in giving guidance on the various sanctions programs, and investigating possible violations of the sanctions programs.

The Designation Process

In October and March of each year the Crime/Narcotics & Western Hemisphere Division at the U.S. Treasury Department's Office of Foreign Assets Control meets with officials from law enforcement, the Department of Defense, and the Intelligence Community to discuss identified targets and solicit additional targets. All identified potential targets are then scrubbed by each agency in its own database for additional information that could possibly be shared for use in the designation process. Each agency is also able to state an objection to a particular designation, if it is felt that the timing of the designation could negatively impact an ongoing operation. Since May 2015, the Treasury Department, through OFAC, has had the authority to designate Kingpins and associated entities on its own. Kingpins are generally referred to as Tier One designees, and associated individuals and legal entities are referred to as Tier Two designees.

OFAC also works with the law enforcement interagency on a real time, case by case basis in order to coordinate the designation process and announcement with law enforcement operations.

The OFAC/DEA Relationship

In 2004 the Office of Foreign Assets Control, an agency of the U.S. Treasury Department, and the Drug Enforcement Administration, an agency of the Department of Justice, entered into a Memorandum of Understanding (MOU) that laid out the process for access to and use of information from DEA's database in its Specially Designated Narcotics Traffickers and Kingpin sanctions programs. Under the MOU, designated OFAC investigators are given permanent certification for entry into DEA headquarters space, and access to the DEA database. The DEA Headquarters office that serves as the point of contact for OFAC is the Office of Global Enforcement, Financial Investigations Section (previously it was the Office of Financial Operations). The process under which DEA information may be disseminated for use in OFAC's investigative reports justifying designation of Kingpins and associated individuals and legal entities is dictated by a Standard Operating Procedure that is overseen and managed by the Financial Investigations Section in DEA Headquarters. Once DEA reports have been thoroughly vetted through this process, the information is disclosed to OFAC by a DEA Senior Executive level official for use in its reports of investigation.

OFAC now also has a permanently assigned investigator at the DEA-led Special Operations Division (SOD). This assignment allows OFAC to have real time access to ongoing investigations of high level foreign narcotics traffickers and money launderers in order to coordinate designation and law enforcement actions against particular targets. DEA also works closely with the OFAC investigators who are permanently assigned to the U.S. embassies in Bogota, Colombia and Mexico City, Mexico, as well as the investigator assigned to the United States Southern Command (U.S. SOUTHCOMM) and the High Intensity Drug Trafficking Area (HIDTA) in Miami, Florida.

OFAC Interaction with U.S. and Foreign Counterparts in the Foreign Arena

Historically, most Specially Designated Narcotics Trafficker (SDNT) and Kingpin Act designations by OFAC have been against Colombian and Mexican cartel leaders, although the numbers of designees outside of these countries have continued to grow, especially in Central and South America. This makes perfect sense, since the cartels in Colombia and Mexico represent the biggest threats to the United States as far as the production and importation of illegal drugs into the American market. OFAC's presence in the U.S. embassies in Bogota, Colombia and Mexico City, Mexico have facilitated the relationships with its U.S. and foreign counterparts in these areas of operation, and the following of the SDNT and Kingpin list of designations by those countries. It also enables the U.S. Ambassadors in those countries to receive real time briefings on impending designations which enables them to stay ahead of and deal with the impact of the political and financial ramifications that those actions will have on their host country.

During my time working for the Organized Crime Section of the Mexican Attorney General's Office in 2009, I witnessed the close working relationship and reliance that that office placed on the OFAC representative assigned to Mexico City in assisting them with their investigations that were initiated as a result of an individual or legal entity being designated by OFAC. I have attended many financial sector conferences in both Mexico and Colombia; and, without reservation, can say that the presentations by the OFAC representatives from the respective embassies and their Washington, DC bosses, were always the most sought after and well attended. I have also attended meetings with financial and business sector leaders in these countries where the impact of OFAC designations was one of the foremost topics of conversation.

Almost all of the countries in the Western Hemisphere now follow the SDNT/Kingpin list. As mentioned previously, the countries that cooperate the most with OFAC are Colombia and Mexico; however, most of the Central and South American countries, cooperate with OFAC.

The Threat of Illicit Drug Proceeds

The Office of National Drug Control Policy (ONDCP), in its February 2014 publication entitled, *What America's Users Spend on Illegal Drugs   2000-2010*, estimated that the illegal drug industry generated in excess of $100 billion per year during the years contained in the study. I doubt that the number has gone down; except for perhaps being replaced to a small degree by revenues generated by State legalized sales of marijuana. Although the exact amount is unknown, a large portion of these proceeds are expatriated each year to foreign sources of drug supply, particularly those located in Latin America. With the ever-increasing presence of Latin American drug cells operating in the U.S. at the wholesale and, at times, retail, distribution levels, I believe that the amount of drug proceeds leaving the U.S. each year is escalating. The cumulative effect of these drug proceeds to negatively impact the stability of democratic states in Latin America and throughout the world, cannot, and should not, be underestimated. These illegal proceeds enable criminal organizations to threaten the stability of governments through corruption, business and financial industries through corruption and unfair competitive advantage, and communities through the violence inherent in the pursuit of control of trafficking routes and safe havens in which to operate.

U.S. law enforcement working with its foreign counterparts cannot always impact the organizations that operate in foreign arenas with traditional methods due to security concerns, weak or corrupt government and legal regimes and processes, inability to operate in certain countries, poor recordkeeping or business practices in tracking financial transactions, and/or lack of extradition agreements. However, these criminal organizations do need access to the financial system and business infrastructure to carry on their operations and hide their wealth. OFAC, through its SDNT/Kingpin sanctions program can reach these otherwise untouchable organizations by crippling them financially and making it impossible to obtain needed services.

The Convergence of Foreign Drug Trafficking Organizations with Foreign Terrorist Organizations

In its 2015 World Drug Report, the United Nations Office of Drugs and Crime stated, *"The nexus between organized crime and terrorism in which illicit drug trafficking appears to play a role poses a serious threat, as emphasized by recent Security Council resolutions calling for redoubled efforts to prevent terrorists from benefiting from transnational organized crime."* DEA investigations and intelligence have linked many of the State Department's designated Foreign Terrorist Organizations (FTOs) to Foreign Drug Trafficking Organizations, at times, as in the cases of the Revolutionary Armed Forces of Colombia, known as the FARC, and Hizbollah, they become, to some extent, one and the same. OFAC, through the Kingpin Act and other sanctions programs which it administers, as well as its close working relationships with DEA and other law enforcement agencies, uses its designation authorities to help strip these FTOs of their ability to earn revenues and purchase operational materials in the international marketplace. In a recent operation, DEA was able to indict and extradite Kassim Tajideen, a fund raiser and money launderer for Hizbollah, for violations relating to a 2009 designation by OFAC under Executive Order 13224, which targets terrorists and those providing support to terrorists or acts of terrorism.

OFAC Sanctions as an Enforcement Tool and Its Impact on Major Foreign Drug Trafficking Organizations

As I mentioned previously, coordinated OFAC sanctions coupled with enforcement takedowns has become a major weapon in DEA's ability to disrupt and dismantle major foreign drug trafficking organizations responsible for the importation of illegal drugs into the United States.

Many successes can be attributed to the designation of individuals and entities since 1995. The most success occurs when a foreign country follows the OFAC designation with economic sanctions and criminal investigations of its own. Colombia is the best example of this. In Colombia, any entity placed on the list is completely shut out from the country's financial system. In Colombia being placed on the "Clinton List" is called "civil death".

The following are but a few of the examples of the impact of the SDNT/Kingpin Act designations by OFAC:

- Perhaps the most notable example of the impact of being placed on the list, is the voluntary surrender and waivers of extradition to the U.S. of Gilberto and Miguel Rodrigez Orejuela, founders and leaders of the Cali (Colombia) Drug Cartel, in 2004 and 2005. The motivation for the Rodrigez Orejuela brothers to voluntarily place themselves in U.S. custody for what could be the remainder of their lives was to have their families removed from the OFAC List.
- The 2004 Kingpin designation of Peruvian Kingpin drug trafficker Fernando Zevallos resulted in the seizure of the US assets belonging to his Peruvian airline and the denial of maintenance services in the US, which put his national airline out of business. The Government of Peru and DEA had been investigating the drug trafficking and money laundering activities of Zevallos in both Peru and the U.S. for more than a decade without success. In support of the OFAC sanctions, DEA and its Peruvian counterparts reinvigorated their investigations; and, Zevallos was subsequently arrested and convicted for drug trafficking in Peru.
- In July 2014, in a coordinated sanctions/enforcement effort with DEA, OFAC designated drug money launderer, Pedro Claver Mejia Salazar and his narcotics money laundering network based in Medellin, Colombia pursuant to the Kingpin Act. OFAC also designated Fredy Alonso Mira Perez, an important underboss in the criminal organization known as La Oficina de Envigado, as well as 10 additional individuals and 14 legal entities, all based in Colombia. OFAC's designation was based on evidence generated by a DEA money laundering investigation. As a direct result of their OFAC designation, both Mejia Salazar and Mira Perez negotiated their voluntary surrender and extradition to the United States, and have since pled guilty to criminal charges in the District of Massachusetts.
- In October 2015, in a coordinated sanctions/enforcement action with DEA, OFAC designated three Honduran businessmen and seven businesses as Specially Designated Narcotics Traffickers pursuant to the Foreign Narcotics Kingpin Designation Act (Kingpin Act) for playing a significant role in international narcotics trafficking. Jaime Rolando Rosenthal Oliva; along with his son, Yani Benjamin Rosenthal Hidalgo; and his nephew, Yankel Antonio Rosenthal Coello, provided money laundering and other services that supported the international narcotics trafficking activities of multiple Central American drug traffickers and their criminal organizations. OFAC's Compliance section coordinated with the US banking sector to freeze the assets of The Rosenthal's Honduran-based bank domiciled in correspondent accounts in the US. In coordination with OFAC's designation, DEA and the U.S. Attorney's Office for the Southern District of New York indicted Jaime Rolando Rosenthal Oliva, Yani Benjamin Rosenthal Hidalgo, and Yankel Antonio Rosenthal Coello, along with a fourth individual, with money laundering in violation of Title 18, United States Code, Section 1956. The Rosenthals were subsequently extradited to the U.S., and all have pled guilty to charges in U.S, District Court in the Southern District of New York. Their multi-billion-dollar

business empire that facilitated the laundering of billions of drug dollars has been completely dismantled. Just as important, the dismantlement of the Rosenthal financial empire has sent shock waves through Central and South America, especially to the wealthy families and businesses that have, to date, aligned themselves with Kingpin drug traffickers in order to cash in on the wealth of these organizations by providing needed financial services.

OFAC Resources

While I cannot speak to the current state of OFAC's resources, I have heard that they are woefully understaffed. This lack of staffing would have an debilitating effect on the availability of OFAC investigators to service the ever-growing request for coordinated investigations. Given the impact that SDNT/Kingpin sanctions have on major foreign drug trafficking organizations and their ability to operate, the return on investment for additional resources for OFAC would be well worth the expenditure.

Suggested Legislative Fixes

Once individuals are placed on the SDNT/Kingpin list, many of them will take steps to conceal their financial dealings and wealth. These transactions, when discovered can form the basis of criminal money laundering violations, and criminal or civil asset forfeiture against the assets involved in the transactions. Depending on where and the manner in which the transactions were conducted, evidence of the source of the funds involved in the transaction may not be obtainable. In these cases, where the individual or legal entity has been designated under a sanction program that draws its authority on the International Emergency Economic Powers Act (IEEPA), the criminal money laundering offense and subsequent forfeiture of the assets can be based on an IEEPA violation. The Kingpin Act (codified as Title 21 United States Code, Sections 1901-1908) does not draw its authority on IEEPA; and, has not, to date, been added to the list of Specified Unlawful Activities (SUAs) listed in the Federal Money Laundering Statute at Title 18 United States Code, Section 1956(c)(7). It would be very helpful to law enforcement if the list of offenses constituting Specified Unlawful Activities under the Federal money laundering statute could be amended to include violations of the Kingpin Act.

Conclusion

Money is the lifeblood of major foreign drug trafficking organizations, and the international financial, business and trade markets are the veins in which this money has to run in order for these organizations to thrive. The Kingpin Act designation authority granted by Congress to the Office of Foreign Assets Control has proven to be an effective and important tool in the toolbox of U.S. law enforcement and regulatory authorities. OFAC has been a vigilant administrator of this authority, as well as a great partner to U.S. law enforcement. The Kingpin Act has had significant impact against the major, foreign drug trafficking organizations as intended by Congress when it passed the initial legislation in 1999.

Mr. Cook. Thank you, Mr. Semesky.

Next let me introduce Mr. David Hall. Mr. Hall is a partner at Wiggin and Dana LLP in the litigation department where he advises clients in a variety of areas but most relevant is his expertise with corporate compliance with the Foreign Corrupt Practices Act. In 2013, Mr. Hall retired from the United States Department of Justice after 23 years as an assistant U.S. attorney.

Mr. Hall, thank you for joining us today, and you are recognized for 5 minutes.

STATEMENT OF MR. DAVID HALL, PARTNER, WIGGIN AND DANA LLP (FORMER PROSECUTOR, U.S. DEPARTMENT OF JUSTICE)

Mr. Hall. Thank you, Mr. Chairman.

Chairman Cook, Ranking Member Sires, and members of the committee, I am very pleased to be here. Thank you very much for giving me the opportunity to testify. I will be summarizing my written statement.

My testimony today will focus on practical sanctions issues from the ground level. In other words, from the point of view of U.S. companies who are required to comply with U.S. sanctions regimes. As you are aware, the Office of Foreign Assets Control administers a number of different sanctions programs. And all of those sanctions programs have in common that they are designed to deal with persons or entities who pose a threat to U.S. national security or U.S. foreign policy objectives.

The Kingpin Act is one point of origin of many for the totality of sanctions programs administered by OFAC. And, taken together, the sanctioned individuals and entities make up the Specially Designated Nationals and Blocked Persons List which is known as the SDN. It is a 1,000 page document that lists more than 5,000 individuals and entities. U.S. persons are generally prohibited from engaging in transactions with any of the individuals or entities on the SDN list.

Today I will address two practical compliance challenges that face U.S. businesses in their role as gatekeepers in complying with the sanctions regimes, including those that originate with the Kingpin Act. One is OFAC's 50 percent rule, which I will describe, and the other is the strict liability standard that applies to all sanctions offenses.

First, the 50 percent rule. OFAC has taken the position that any entity that is owned 50 percent or more in the aggregate, directly or indirectly, by one or more blocked persons, is itself considered to be a blocked entity even if that entity is not itself named on the SDN list. The question is: How does a widget maker in Wisconsin deal with that? As you are aware, many sanctioned individuals, including kingpins exert enormous effort to remain invisible, and, in part, to avoid U.S. sanctions. How does a widget maker crack that code?

Through the 50 percent rule, the government has outsourced the fundamental national security function to the private sector. And this is effective, in my opinion, in reducing government accountability but is not effective in terms of achieving the goals of U.S. sanctions programs. This is because U.S. businesses ordinarily do not have the resources and the ability to gain the kind of granular information that is necessary to understand the ownership structure of every business partner or customer.

In contrast, the U.S. Government does have access to that kind of information through the intel community and through law enforcement agencies. Since the government has the most reliable and efficient means of making those determinations, in my opinion, the government should do that and should list all sanctioned entities instead of leaving it up to the private sector to identify 50 percent partners.

The second issue I wanted to address briefly is the strict liability standard. The sanctions regime seems simple. The government publishes a list of sanctioned individuals. U.S. companies have to read that list and can't do business with those entities. Sometimes it is exactly that simple but not always. Companies employ search protocols in order to determine whether or not they are dealing with sanctioned individuals and entities. But these search protocols often yield false positives or near positives. There are a lot of sources for these errors, including common names, names with multiple spellings, of course misspellings, the fact that foreign language names need to be translated and are sometimes mistranslated, not to mention cultural differences in naming conventions. As a result, U.S. businesses are left with a question: How close is too close?

Now, why is this such a big problem? Because the OFAC sanctions are administered according to a strict liability standard, which means that good faith is not a defense. So a company could be doing everything in its power to comply with OFAC sanctions, but if it accidentally violates those sanctions, then it is still liable and the only question is: What will the penalty be? The government does take good-faith compliance into account when determining penalties, but, in the end, it is up to the government. In my opinion, this is not fair. But, in addition, it is not an effective means of enforcing sanctions.

So I have two recommendations. One is abolish the 50 percent rule. And the other is I think that a good-faith exception to the strict liability standard should be established. This will enable the government to focus its attention on companies that are not acting in good faith which is really the focus of any law enforcement enterprise.

Thank you. I look forward to your questions.

[The prepared statement of Mr. Hall follows:]

PREPARED TESTIMONY
of
David L. Hall
Partner, Wiggin and Dana
Before the
Subcommittee on the Western Hemisphere
Committee on Foreign Affairs
United States House of Representatives

"Examining the Effectiveness of the Kingpin Designation Act in the Western Hemisphere"
November 8, 2017

Chairman Cook, Ranking Members, and Members of the Committee:

Thank you for the opportunity to appear before you today for this hearing "Examining the Effectiveness of the Kingpin Designation Act in the Western Hemisphere."

My name is David L. Hall, and I am a partner at the law firm of Wiggin and Dana LLP. Prior to joining Wiggin and Dana, I served as an Assistant United States Attorney with the Department of Justice for 23 years. I am also a retired naval intelligence officer, having served in the Navy for thirty years, active and reserve.

Opening Remarks

The Office of Foreign Assets Control ("OFAC") administers numerous sanctions programs focused on foreign countries, rogue regimes, terrorist organizations, criminal organizations, and other persons and entities that pose a threat to U.S national security and U.S. foreign policy objectives. While some of these programs place prohibitions on specified activities with persons and entities in targeted foreign countries, others, like the Foreign Narcotics Kingpin Designation Act (the "Kingpin Act") target individuals and entities involved in criminal enterprises such as narcotics trafficking. Collectively, these individuals and entities make up the Specially Designated Nationals and Blocked Persons List (the "SDN List"). The SDN List is a 1,054 page document identifying more than 5,000 individuals and entities blocked under an OFAC sanctions program.[1] With rare exceptions, U.S. persons are prohibited from engaging in transactions with any individuals or entities on the SDN List.

The objective of the Kingpin Act, as with other sanctions programs, is to cut off known bad actors (in this case foreign narcotics traffickers and their criminal organizations) from access to U.S. financial markets, thus crippling their ability to reap the rewards of their criminal actions and to weaken their ability to fund their criminal enterprise. The strength of these programs lies in the Government's ability to ensure that non-government actors in the United States, primarily financial institutions and U.S. businesses, act as gatekeepers to prevent these bad actors from moving funds, making investments, and purchasing goods and services. While law enforcement agencies are responsible for apprehending

---

[1] In addition to the SDN List, OFAC administers a list of persons and entities subject to Sectoral Sanctions (Russia/Ukraine Sanctions Program) and Foreign Sanctions Evaders. The Department of Commerce similarly publishes a list of entities and individuals subject to export restrictions regulated by the Bureau of Industry and Security ("BIS"). OFAC maintains a Consolidated Sanctions List which includes the following data files: Foreign Sanctions Evaders (FSE) List; Sectoral Sanctions Identifications (SSI) List; Palestinian Legislative Council (NS-PLC) List; The List of Foreign Financial Institutions Subject to Part 561 (the Part 561 List); Non-SDN Iranian Sanctions Act (NS-ISA) List; and the List of Persons Identified as Blocked Solely Pursuant to Executive Order 13599 (the 13599 List).

the bad actors and stopping the movement of narcotics into the United States, OFAC aims for the purse-strings of these criminal organizations.

From the perspective of U.S. businesses, the Kingpin Act does not impose compliance burdens substantially different from those of other sanctions programs. Today, I will address practical compliance challenges that U.S. businesses, in their role as gatekeepers, face in navigating U.S. sanctions programs overall, including those originating with the Kingpin Act.

As a former prosecutor and a former naval intelligence officer, I consider sanctions programs to be important arrows in the national security quiver. My comments are offered in the hope that the effectiveness and fairness of these programs can be improved.

Businesses face many challenges in sanctions compliance, and my testimony focuses on just two. First, I will address OFAC's "50 Percent Rule," which imposes significant burdens and undue risk on U.S. business – and also subverts the purpose of the rule itself. Second, I will attempt to shed some light on the practical challenges companies face in attempting to comply with U.S. sanctions programs, in order to demonstrate the pitfalls of a strict liability approach to violations of U.S. sanctions.

The OFAC "50 Percent Rule"

Property blocked pursuant to an Executive Order or regulations administered by OFAC is broadly defined to include any property or interest in property, tangible or intangible, including "present, future or contingent interests."[2] OFAC has taken the position that an entity owned 50 percent or more in the aggregate, directly or indirectly, by one or more blocked persons is itself considered to be blocked **even where that entity is not on the SDN List**.[3]

How is a widget manufacturer in Wisconsin supposed to deal with this? As you are aware, many sanctioned individuals -- including Kingpins – exert significant effort to become invisible, precisely in order to avoid the effects of U.S. sanctions. These bad actors often hide behind front companies, with complex and anonymous ownership structures. As a practical matter, most U.S. companies, particularly small businesses, do not have the resources to uncover the ownership structures of all their customers and business partners. This is particularly true when their customers – for good reasons or bad– want that information to be confidential.

Placing the burden on U.S. businesses to uncover these connections is not fair or practical. Through the 50 Percent Rule, which tasks U.S. businesses with determining whether any potential business transactions involve entities owned 50 percent or more by a blocked party, the government has outsourced a fundamental national security function to the private sector. This is effective in reducing government accountability, but is not effective as a means of accomplishing the goals of U.S. sanctions programs.

The 50 Percent Rule almost guarantees that the U.S. Government will fail in achieving its own objectives. U.S. businesses ordinarily do not have access to the kind of granular information that would

---

[2] *See Revised Guidance on Entities Owned by Persons Whose Property and Interests in Property are Blocked,* Department of Treasury (Aug. 13, 2014) ("OFAC 50 Percent Rule Guidance"), available at https://www.treasury.gov/resource-center/sanctions/Documents/licensing_guidance.pdf. Specifically, the Kingpin Act defines blocked property to mean "any account or property subject to [a blocking action under the Act] held in [the name of a designated person], or in which a [designated person] has an interest, and with respect to which payments, transfers, exportations, withdrawals, or other dealings may not be made or effected except pursuant to an authorization or license from the Office of Foreign Assets Control authorizing such action." 31 C.F.R. § 598.301.

[3] OFAC 50 Percent Rule Guidance (Aug. 13, 2014).

enable them to determine 50 percent ownership of customers and business partners. Furthermore, even if a U.S. business is able to identify a secret owner of an entity, that information is not typically shared, so the rest of the private sector -- and the government itself – does not benefit from that discovery.

In addition to having access to the same publicly available information on which U.S. businesses must rely, the U.S. Government has access to intelligence and law enforcement information and resources dedicated to identifying entities and individuals acting for or on behalf of targeted countries and individuals. Since the government has more reliable and efficient means to identify downstream ownership, it should identify and sanction the appropriate parties.

Compliance Challenges and Strict Liability

The sanctions regime seems simple. The government publishes a list of names. U.S. businesses are charged with the duty of reading the list and blocking transactions with anyone on the list. And sometimes it is exactly that simple. But not always.

Search protocols frequently result in false positives or near positives.[4] This is particularly true in the case of common names, or in the case of names with multiple spellings. The situation is further exacerbated by foreign language and translation issues, including transliteration of names from non-Roman alphabets, identifying surnames versus given names, or cultural differences in naming conventions. A number of screening tools are available to businesses, which offer analytics and other support services to reduce uncertainty and provide more accurate results. However, in many cases, determining whether there is a true match between a potential customer or business partner and a designated party is based on a judgment call made with incomplete information. It is in these areas of uncertainty that businesses take on significant risk, which they cannot reduce by further research because they do not have access to the kind of information that would definitively resolve the matter. U.S. businesses are thus left with the question of how close is too close?

OFAC offers its own free search database, which allows users to search against several OFAC sanctions lists. Users can run searches for "exact matches" or employ fuzzy logic to capture a wider range of potential matches.[5] OFAC does not recommend any particular approach or search strategy, but rather advises that users "must make their own determinations based upon their own internal risk assessments and established practices."[6]

---

[4] A recent informal testing of several third party screening vendors resulted in vastly divergent false hit rates. The test involved a sample of over 100 entries consisting of a pre-determined mix of previously confirmed denied parties (SDNs) and unlisted persons. The likelihood of false positives (where an unlisted person appears as a potential match to an SDN) ranged from approximately 2% to 82%. The likelihood of false negatives (where an SDN match was missed) ranged from approximately 9% to 75%. The false hit rate increased dramatically when misspellings or common transliteration errors were introduced.

[5] OFAC has published frequently asked questions (FAQs) regarding how its search database works and how scores are calculated. These FAQs are available at https://www.treasury.gov/resource-center/sanctions/SDN-List/Pages/fuzzy_logic.aspx.

[6] *Id.* In some instances, a company may determine that its risk profile does not warrant implementing an expensive third party screening program. Even if that determination is made based on a good faith evaluation of the company's risk of doing business with prohibited parties, the company is still subject to heavy penalties. In a recent OFAC enforcement action, a retail jewelry business entered a settlement agreeing to pay $333,800 as a result of engaging in four transactions involving the shipment of jewelry to an SDN identified under the Kingpin Sanctions. *See* Enforcement Information for September 26, 2017, available at https://www.treasury.gov/resource-center/sanctions/CivPen/Pages/civpen-index2.aspx.

How does this work in practice? By way of illustration, Muhammad Ali – "the Greatest of All Time" -- is a 100% match. Another example: a very nice Georgetown bakery is an 84% match to an entity recently designated under the Kingpin sanctions. This does not mean that there is an 84% likelihood that the bakery and the Kingpin are connected, but rather that they have 84% similarity based on the algorithms of OFAC's search tool. What is the Wisconsin widget maker to do with this information? Further research might resolve the issue, as in the case of Muhammad Ali. But it might not, illustrating how easily a business can be faced with the conundrum of how, with incomplete information, to meet its responsibility to determine if a business partner is a bad actor.

Why is this such a big problem? Because a violation of OFAC regulations is a strict liability offense and the maximum penalties are substantial.[7] So, regardless of a company's good faith intention to comply with the law, it can be held liable for any transaction with a designated party, and subjected to severe penalties. In making penalty determinations, the government does consider mitigating factors such as an effective compliance program, the lack of willfulness, proactive disclosures to the government, and cooperation with an investigation. But the company is still liable, and, in the end, the penalty is up to the government.

In theory, it makes sense to impose a strict liability standard on a program designed to protect our national security. That's because national security is important, existentially so. But as a practical matter, the strict liability standard cannot itself guarantee enhanced national security. And it can be brutally unfair. Consider the small company that fails – after trying in good faith -- to determine that a sanctioned person is a 50 percent owner, through an anonymous front company, of one of its customers. Should that company be strictly liable for fines and penalties? I don't think so. I don't think that's fair.

Recommendations

I was trained in the Navy that every problem has a solution. In that spirit, I offer these recommendations:

- Abolish the 50 Percent Rule. Put the burden of identifying sanctioned individuals and entities on the government. Or, in the alternative, create a safe harbor where a company can submit names to the government for review.
- Create a good faith exception to the strict liability standard. This will allow compliant companies that are doing their best to satisfy the requirements of sanctions programs to avoid unfair penalties. And it will preserve the ability of the government to pursue penalties against companies that are not acting in good faith – which is the real problem the government should address.

Thank you very much for your attention.

---

[7] The maximum civil penalty for an OFAC penalty under the International Emergency Economic Powers Act ("IEEPA") is currently $289,238 (or twice the amount of the underlying transaction, whichever is greater). 82 Fed. Reg. 10434 (Feb. 10, 2017). The maximum civil penalty under the Kingpin Act is $1,437,153 per violation. 31 CFR 598.701.

Mr. COOK. Thank you, Mr. Hall.

Next let me introduce Dr. Emanuele Ottolenghi. Close?

Mr. OTTOLENGHI. Very close. Perfect.

Mr. COOK. This gentleman is a senior fellow at the Foundation for the Defense of Democracies and an expert at its Center on Sanctions and Illicit Finance focusing on Iran.

Sir, I want to thank you for joining us today. You are now recognized for 5 minutes.

STATEMENT OF EMANUELE OTTOLENGHI, PH.D., SENIOR FELLOW, CENTER ON SANCTIONS AND ILLICIT FINANCE, FOUNDATION FOR DEFENSE OF DEMOCRACIES

Mr. OTTOLENGHI. Chairman Cook, allow me first to congratulate you on your recent appointment as the new chairman of this subcommittee.

Mr. COOK. Thank you.

Mr. OTTOLENGHI. Mr. Chairman, Ranking Member Sires, members of the subcommittee, I thank you for the opportunity to testify.

Hezbollah's growing involvement in transnational organized crime is a multibillion dollar global enterprise endorsed and coordinated by the group's top leaders not a side business operated by greedy operatives gone rogue. Increasing quantities of cocaine invade the U.S. and Europe from Latin America. Cocaine consumption is as much a national epidemic as opioids and Hezbollah helps make it available to U.S. consumers. Take the recent extradition from Paraguay to Miami of suspected Hezbollah drug trafficker Ali Chamas. Court documents show that he was part of a larger network likely based in Colombia. At the time of his arrest, he was conspiring to export as many as 100 kilograms of cocaine a month to the U.S. by air cargo.

The U.S. has remarkably sharp and effective tools to counteract Hezbollah's terrifying threat, though it is not always using them as vigorously as it should. To illustrate the problem, let me offer two examples which I discuss at length in my written statement.

In 2011, the DEA indicted Ayman Joumaa, a Lebanese-Colombian dual national who operated a global network of companies laundering drug money from Mexican and Colombian cartels to the tune of $200 million a month. Joumaa worked with Hezbollah as the kingpin in one of its many global networks. A DEA official discussing the case said that Hezbollah operated like "the Gambinos on steroids." As the combination of numerous coordinated actions which included kingpin designations, the Joumaa case illustrates the effect of the Kingpin Act.

Hezbollah's use of the tri-border area of Argentina, Brazil, and Paraguay, or TBA, both to launder money from illicit traffics, and as a staging ground for its drug runners shows you a sanctions policy current shortcomings. In my written statement I offer evidence of the TBA's importance too Hezbollah's global illicit trade. Lack of U.S.-sanction enforcement against Hezbollah TBA operatives since their terror finance designation in 2004 and 2006, coupled with light or no penalties for sanctioned violators, have allowed Hezbollah to strengthen its presence and increase revenues from illicit traffics including cocaine.

Unless U.S. sanctions are constantly updated and vigorously enforced, targeted individuals and entities can soon elude them and shrug off their effects, especially if they can count on local corrupt authorities to collude with them as it is the case with Hezbollah and the TBA.

Both successful cases I mention in my written statement involved a sanctions and a law enforcement component. They also relied on unprecedented intelligence sharing and interagency coordination, cooperation with foreign law enforcement and intel agencies from allied countries, and the reliance on a panoply of tools drawn from the sanctions arsenal and in the Joumma case, the PATRIOT Act as well.

The Kingpin Act shares the same strengths and limitations of other sanctions programs. When combined with other tools and leverage as a basis for prosecution is very effective. That is why I strongly recommend that the U.S. administration designate Hezbollah and its senior leadership as both a transnational criminal organization and a global kingpin. U.S. sanctions occasionally stumble upon the reluctance or refusal by regional governments to cooperate. No Latin American country has so far designated Hezbollah as a terrorist organization. Its terror financiers are not being prosecuted as such. U.S. requests to arrest, prosecute, and extradite them might be easier if they are under kingpin designations as well. Kingpin designations can also punish Hezbollah's enablers. Were the U.S. to target the Latin American financial institution involved in facilitating Hezbollah's drug transactions, the impact would be devastating.

Global Magnitsky Act designations should also be considered for those whom Hezbollah bribes and corrupts for access, influence, favors, and collusion in its criminal activities.

Requests that the President investigate cases of corruption by foreign officials can come from chairpersons and ranking members of relevant committees in Congress. Such requests would put the spotlight on narcoterrorism's worst enablers. Kingpin designations have had salutary effects. They have named and shamed individuals, companies, and organizations, led to asset seizures, cut off their entities from the U.S. financial systems, nudged U.S. allies and the global corporate and financial sectors into compliance. Nevertheless, there are enough countries that disagree with, or disregard, U.S. policy. Hezbollah operatives find a haven where U.S. sanctions alone have limited reach.

And, finally, Mr. Chairman, to run an effective policy, we need people and resources in place. First and foremost, the U.S. urgently needs a new DEA administrator with the vision and experience to go after transnational criminal organizations such as Hezbollah and with the skills to coordinate government agencies, navigate bureaucracy, and build friendships and international alliances.

OFAC also cannot work cases through the sytem without access to more resources that can enable the bureaucracy to work faster and cast its net wider.

Now, these are just some of my recommendations, Mr. Chairman, and I very much look forward to your questions. Thank you.

[The prepared statement of Mr. Ottolenghi follows:]

CONGRESSIONAL TESTIMONY: FOUNDATION FOR DEFENSE OF DEMOCRACIES

House Foreign Affairs Committee
Subcommittee on the Western Hemisphere

Examining the Effectiveness of the Kingpin Designation Act in the Western Hemisphere

DR. EMANUELE OTTOLENGHI

Senior Fellow
*Foundation for Defense of Democracies,
Center on Sanctions and Illicit Finance*

Washington, DC
November 8, 2017

www.defenddemocracy.org

Emanuele Ottolenghi   November 8, 2017

Chairman Cook, allow me first to congratulate you on your recent appointment as the new chairman of this subcommittee. Mr. Chairman, Ranking Member Sires, members of the subcommittee, thank you for the opportunity to testify on behalf of the Foundation for Defense of Democracies and its Center on Sanctions and Illicit Finance.

In 2011, the U.S. Drug Enforcement Administration (DEA) indicted Ayman Saied Joumaa, a Lebanese-Colombian dual national whose global network of companies operating out of Latin America, West Africa, and Lebanon laundered money for Mexican and Colombian cartels to the tune of $200 million a month of drug proceeds.[1] Joumaa worked with Hezbollah as the kingpin in one of many networks Hezbollah runs globally to sustain its financial needs. When his case came to light, the *New York Times* quoted a DEA official as saying that Hezbollah operated like "the Gambinos on steroids."[2]

The United States cannot continue to combat a threat of such magnitude unless it leverages all its tools of statecraft in a combined, sustained, and coordinated fashion. Over the past decade, Hezbollah's terror finance outside Lebanon has evolved from a relatively small fundraising operation involving trade-based money laundering and charitable donations into a multi-billion dollar global criminal enterprise.

Increasing quantities of Schedule 2 drugs like cocaine invade the U.S. from Latin America, adding fuel to the opioid pandemic that has already cost so many lives.[3] Cocaine consumption is as much a national epidemic as opioids, Mr. Chairman, and Hezbollah helps make it available to U.S. consumers.

This makes Hezbollah, its senior leadership, and its numerous operatives involved in running illicit drug-trafficking and money-laundering operations on a global scale the perfect candidates for Kingpin and Transnational Crime Organization designations, in addition to the terrorism and terror finance designations already in place.

The U.S. government has, over the years, developed remarkably sharp and effective tools to counteract Hezbollah's terror finance threat, but is not using them as vigorously as it should. The Kingpin Act is one such instrument. But like all other instruments of statecraft, its impact would be much greater if used consistently and in conjunction with other tools. The challenge for Congress, the executive branch, the intelligence community, and law enforcement agencies is to leverage these tools in a manner that will outsmart Hezbollah and disrupt its cash flows enough to inflict irreparable damage to the terror group's finances.

---

[1] U.S. Department of the Treasury, Press Release, "Treasury Targets Major Lebanese-Based Drug Trafficking and Money Laundering Network," January 26, 2011. (https://www.treasury.gov/press-center/press-releases/Pages/tg1035.aspx); see also: U.S. Department of the Treasury, Press Release, "U.S. Charges Alleged Lebanese Drug Kingpin with Laundering Drug Proceeds for Mexican and Colombian Drug Cartels," December 13, 2011. (https://www.justice.gov/archive/usao/vae/news/2011/12/20111213joumaanr.html)
[2] Jo Becker, "Beirut Bank Seen as a Hub of Hezbollah's Financing," *The New York Times*, December 13, 2011. (http://www.nytimes.com/2011/12/14/world/middleeast/beirut-bank-seen-as-a-hub-of-hezbollahs-financing.html)
[3] Nick Miroff, "American cocaine use is way up. Colombia's coca boom may be why," *The Washington Post*, March 4, 2017. (https://www.washingtonpost.com/news/worldviews/wp/2017/03/04/colombias-coca-boom-is-showing-up-on-u-s-streets/?utm_term=.d370be3ebe9c)

Emanuele Ottolenghi   November 8, 2017

In pursuit of this goal, America needs to better coordinate the application and enforcement of all instruments available from the formidable toolbox created over the past two decades by legislation and executive orders, including leveraging Executive Orders 13581 and 13773 on combating transnational organized crime, Executive Order 13224 on combating sources of terror finance, the 1999 Foreign Narcotics Kingpin Designation Act, the 2015 Hezbollah International Financing Prevention Act (HIFPA), the Global Magnitsky Human Rights Accountability Act of 2016, and soon the Hezbollah International Financing Prevention Act Amendment of 2017, which is now awaiting reconciliation between its House and Senate versions and which will, once approved, expand on HIFPA.

In doing so, it should focus significantly on the Western Hemisphere, where Hezbollah's global footprint, especially in Latin America, is most menacing.

Hezbollah's regional operations are part of a global network of illicit financial and commercial enterprises whose goal is to fund Hezbollah's activities in the Middle East. Where and when needed, these networks can also be activated to provide logistical support to operatives engaged in planning terror attacks. The United States therefore needs to think and act globally to disrupt Hezbollah's illicit finance networks. Latin America is a very good place to start doing that.

In the remainder of my testimony, I will discuss evidence demonstrating the magnitude of the threat posed by Hezbollah's terror finance to the national security of the United States. I will also provide evidence of the high-ranking nature of Hezbollah's operatives in Latin America – a sure sign of the importance of Hezbollah's Latin American networks to the organization's budget. And I will discuss the impact of U.S. policy and actions on disrupting Hezbollah's terror finance activities. The evidence I am presenting today, hopefully, will highlight both strengths and weaknesses of present U.S. policy and offer ways to improve results.

HEZBOLLAH'S LATIN AMERICAN NETWORKS: DEFINING THE PROBLEM

Hezbollah's involvement in Latin America's drug trade is significant and expanding. The group – often referred to as the "A-Team" of international terrorism – has reportedly formed partnerships with several of the region's most notorious crime syndicates, including Mexico's Zetas,[4] Columbia's FARC,[5] and Brazil's Primeiro Comando de la Capital.[6] Drug trafficking cases involving Lebanese with suspected ties to Hezbollah are increasingly frequent. Evidence indicates that Hezbollah has ties that span the entire illicit narcotics supply chain. U.S. sanctions, as well as court cases in the United States and overseas, have targeted Hezbollah-linked operatives acting as

---

[4] Terence Rosenthal, "Los Zetas and Hezbollah, a Deadly Alliance of Terror and Vice," *Center for Security Policy*, July 10, 2013. (http://www.centerforsecuritypolicy.org/2013/07/10/los-zetas-and-hezbollah-a-deadly-alliance-of-terror-and-vice/)
[5] Jo Becker, "Beirut Bank Seen as a Hub of Hezbollah's Financing," *The New York Times*, December 13, 2011. (http://www.nytimes.com/2011/12/14/world/middleeast/beirut-bank-seen-as-a-hub-of-hezbollahs-financing.html)
[6] Kyra Gurney, "Police Documents Reveal 'Hezbollah Ties' to Brazil's PCC," *Insight Crime*, November 10, 2014. (http://www.insightcrime.org/news-briefs/police-documents-hezbollah-ties-brazil-pcc)

Emanuele Ottolenghi   November 8, 2017

logistical and financial service providers,[7] traffickers,[8] drug barons,[9] distributors,[10] and, most recently, suppliers of precursor chemicals used to refine cocaine.[11] It seems only a matter of time before Hezbollah-run drug labs emerge, too – the kind that have long been at the center of the group's operations in Lebanon's Bekaa Valley.[12]

Hezbollah's operatives in Latin America play a central role in a new landscape where drug and human trafficking, gun running, illicit cigarette trade, trade-based money laundering, and terror finance can no longer be treated as distinct phenomena. Terror organizations like Hezbollah help criminal cartels and local mafias move merchandise to their markets. They then launder revenues through sales of consumer goods. The profits fund terrorist activities.

Hezbollah's services come with a fee – and the money collected for acting as the cartels' middlemen fuels their war machine in Syria, their arms buildup in South Lebanon, and their efforts to carry out terrorist plots abroad. Targets include both Latin America and the U.S., as illustrated by at least two known, recent cases.

First, Peruvian authorities arrested a suspected Hezbollah member, Muhammad Amadar, in October 2014.[13] Though his trial did not lead to a conviction for terrorism – in April 2017 he was sentenced to six years in prison for falsifying his immigration papers[14] – Amadar was identified by the U.S. Department of the Treasury as a Hezbollah operative and sanctioned in 2016.[15] According to Matthew Levitt of the Washington Institute for Near East Policy, Amadar's handler for operational planning was Salman al-Reda, aka Salman Raouf Salman, the Lebanese-Colombian dual national and Hezbollah member who was the on-the-ground coordinator for the 1994 terror

[7] "Interagency Cooperation on Tri-Border Area," *Wikileaks Cable: 07Asuncion688_a*, August 20, 2007. (https://wikileaks.org/plusd/cables/07ASUNCION688_a.html)
[8] Opinion, *United States of America v. Yahya Zaitar*, No. 08-123 (RMC) (D.D.C. filed January 13, 2015). (https://www.courtlistener.com/pdf/2015/01/13/united_states_v._zaitar.pdf)
[9] U.S. Department of the Treasury, Press Release, "Recent OFAC Actions," June 1, 2006. (https://www.treasury.gov/resource-center/sanctions/OFAC-Enforcement/Pagés/20060601.aspx)
[10] "Libanés cae con 500 kilos de cocaína en aeropuerto Guaraní (Lebanese caught with 500 kilos of cocaine in Guarani airport)," *La Nacion* (Argentina), August 19, 2016. (http://www.lanacion.com.py/2016/08/19/cocaina-aeropuerto-guarani-minga-guazu/)
[11] Daniel Gallo, "Acopiaban más de 80 toneladas de precursores a metros de la frontera (Collected more than 80 tons of precursors a few meters from the border)," *La Nacion* (Argentina), July 25, 2016. (http://www.lanacion.com.ar/1921575-acopiaban-mas-de-80-toneladas-de-precursores-a-metros-de-la-frontera)
[12] Rebecca Collard, "Lebanon's drug lords say they are ready to join the fight against ISIS," *Public Radio International*, January 6, 2015. (https://www.pri.org/stories/2015-01-06/lebanons-drug-lords-say-theyre-ready-join-fight-against-isis)
[13] "Presunto miembro de Hezbollah fue detenido en Surquillo (Alleged member of Hezbollah was detained in Surquillo)," *RPP Noticias* (Peru), October 29, 2014. (http://rpp.pe/lima/actualidad/presunto-miembro-de-hezbollah-fue-detenido-en-surquillo-noticia-737561)
[14] "Absuelven a Libanes acusado de terrorismo detenido en Surquillo (Lebanese accused of terrorism detained in Surquillo is acquitted)," *El Comercio* (Peru), April 21, 2017. (https://elcomercio.pe/peru/absuelven-libanes-acusado-terrorismo-detenido-surquillo-415800)
[15] U.S. Department of the Treasury, "Counter-Terrorism Designations," October 20, 2016. (https://www.treasury.gov/resource-center/sanctions/OFAC-Enforcement/Pagés/20161020.aspx)

Emanuele Ottolenghi   November 8, 2017

attack on the AMIA building in Buenos Aires.[16] Amadar met al-Reda numerous times to plan the attack in Peru, which was eventually foiled by his arrest.

On June 1, 2017, U.S. law enforcement authorities arrested Ali Kourani and Samer el Debek, both U.S. citizens, for scouting targets in Panama and the United States, with a view of plotting terror attacks. Potential targets included critical infrastructure such as the Panama Canal, and military and law enforcement facilities in the U.S. Both individuals were identified as members of Hezbollah's Islamic Jihad Organization, a Hezbollah component in charge of overseas operations.[17]

Hezbollah has not only been involved in plotting terror attacks and facilitating drug traffic. It has also fueled the type of rampant corruption that the Global Magnitsky Act was designed to counter. To ensure its operations' success in the region, Hezbollah operatives in Latin America routinely buy off local politicians, judges, prosecutors, immigration authorities, border control officers, customs officials, and police. They enjoy considerable political access and impunity from justice, thanks to corrupt and conniving political elites in key Latin American countries. These operatives also rely on a vast network of complicit expatriates who collude in illicit and highly profitable schemes, motivated by a varying mix of familial loyalties, greed, religious zeal, patriotism, and opportunism.

Hezbollah's documented involvement in drug trafficking, the illicit cigarette and tobacco trade,[18] illicit timber[19] and blood diamond trades,[20] counterfeit and pirated goods,[21] and possibly in human and organ trafficking[22] is not the work of rogue members or of people who, while possibly sympathizing and even actively making charitable donations to Hezbollah, are not part of the terror group.

Mr. Chairman, Hezbollah's growing involvement in global crime is not a side business operated by greedy operatives gone rogue. It is part of a deliberate strategy endorsed by Hezbollah's highest authorities and managed in hierarchical and highly structured fashion through Hezbollah's

---

[16] Matthew Levitt, "Hezbollah's Growing Threat Against U.S. National Security Interests in the Middle East," *The Washington Institute for Near East Policy*, March 22, 2016.
(https://www.washingtoninstitute.org/uploads/Documents/testimony/LevittTestimony20160322.pdf)
[17] U.S. Department of Justice, Press Release, "Two Men Arrested for Terrorist Activities on Behalf of Hizbullah's Islamic Jihad Organization," June 8, 2017. (https://www.justice.gov/opa/pr/two-men-arrested-terrorist-activities-behalf-hizballahs-islamic-jihad-organization)
[18] A 2016 report published by Israel's ministry of health on tobacco issued in Israel states that "illicit trade of tobacco constitutes an important source of funding for Hezbollah." Israel Ministry of Health, " דו"ח שר הבריאות על העישון בישראל 2015 (Report of the Minister of Health on Smoking in Israel)," May 2016, page 134.
[19] "US Consumers Buying Millions of Dollars-Worth of Luxury Timber Linked to Hezbollah Financiers, Global Witness Reveals," *Global Witness*, February 9, 2017. (https://www.globalwitness.org/en/press-releases/us-consumers-buying-millions-dollars-worth-luxury-timber-linked-hezbollah-financiers-global-witness-reveals/)
[20] U.S. Department of the Treasury, Press Release, "Treasury Targets Hizballah Financial Network," May 27, 2009. (https://www.treasury.gov/press-center/press-releases/Pages/tg149.aspx). According to Treasury, the businessman targeted in their designation, Kassim Tajideen, was arrested in Belgium in connection to "fraud, money laundering and diamond smuggling."
[21] Gregory F. Treverton, "Film Piracy, Organized Crime, and Terrorism," *RAND Corporation*, October 31, 2008. (https://www.rand.org/content/dam/rand/pubs/monographs/2009/RAND_MG742.pdf)
[22] Matthew Levitt, "South of the Border, a Threat from Hezbollah," *The Journal of International Security Affairs*, May 15, 2013. (https://www.washingtoninstitute.org/uploads/Documents/opeds/Levitt20130515-JISA.pdf)

Emanuele Ottolenghi

Executive Council and the External Security Organization's Business Affairs Component, which acts under the directions of the Executive Council.

Still, important questions, as far as policymaking is concerned, are: How much does Hezbollah earn? Does Hezbollah still mainly rely on Iran for its funding? How large is its overall operating budget, and how much of it comprises revenue from Hezbollah's illicit activities overseas?

The U.S. Department of the Treasury thought that overseas contributions to Hezbollah from illicit trade were significant enough to pursue. In 2004,[23] and then again in 2006,[24] it sanctioned Hezbollah operatives in the Tri-Border Area of Argentina, Brazil and Paraguay, or TBA, who were engaged in a variety of criminal activities to finance the terror group. Their activities included drug trafficking, currency counterfeiting, and racketeering.

At the time, it was estimated that revenue generated through trade-based money laundering and other illicit activities in the TBA yielded roughly $10 million for Hezbollah, out of an estimated budget of $100 million a year. A 2004 Naval War College study assessed that "Hezbollah, whose annual operating budget is roughly one hundred million dollars, raises roughly a tenth of that in Paraguay."[25] A 2009 RAND study doubled the estimate of money raised mainly in the TBA to $20 million.[26] Regardless of the accuracy of these estimates, Hezbollah's operating expenses have mushroomed since the early 2000s. Hezbollah's financial needs have grown significantly since then, mainly due to the damage suffered in its 2006 war with Israel and, since 2011, due to its deepening involvement in the Syrian civil war.[27] Iran's funding has grown along with Hezbollah's needs, but the ebbs and flows of Iranian support,[28] combined with pressure from U.S. measures that began hitting Hezbollah's finances in Lebanon in 2015, have meant that Hezbollah's reliance on alternative funding streams has become more critical to its operational needs.

After the 2006 war with Israel, Hezbollah's highest authorities instructed their followers to engage in criminal activity to restore the organization's fighting abilities. Multiple media and law enforcement sources confirm this religious endorsement.[29] According to U.S. law enforcement

---

[23] U.S. Department of the Treasury, Press Release, "Treasury Designates Islamic Extremist, Two Companies Supporting Hizballah in Tri-Border Area," June 10, 2004. (https://www.treasury.gov/press-center/press-releases/Pagés/js1720.aspx)

[24] U.S. Department of the Treasury, Press Release, "Treasury Targets Hizballah Fundraising Network in the Triple Frontier of Argentina, Brazil, and Paraguay," December 6, 2006. (https://www.treasury.gov/press-center/press-releases/Pagés/hp190.aspx)

[25] Paul D. Taylor, "Latin American Security Challenges: A Collaborative Inquiry from North and South," *Naval War College Newport Papers*, accessed May 6, 2017. (https://www.usnwc.edu/Publications/Naval-War-College-Press/-Newport-Papers/Documents/21-pdf.aspx)

[26] Gregory F. Treverton et al., "Film Piracy, Organized Crime, and Terrorism," *RAND Corporation*, 2009. (http://www.rand.org/content/dam/rand/pubs/monographs/2009/RAND_MG742.pdf)

[27] Matthew Levitt, "The Crackdown on Hezbollah's Financial Network," *The Wall Street Journal*, June 27, 2016. (https://blogs.wsj.com/washwire/2016/01/27/the-crackdown-on-hezbollahs-financing-network/)

[28] Oren Kessler & Rubert Sutton, "Hezbollah threatened by Iran's Financial Woes," *World Affairs Journal*, June 3, 2014. (http://www.worldaffairsjournal.org/article/hezbollah-threatened-iran%E2%80%99s-financial-woes)

[29] Marco Vernaschi, "The Cocaine Coast," *Virginia Quarterly Online*, Winter 2010. (http://www.vqronline.org/essay/cocaine-coast). According to this report, "Most of Hezbollah's support comes from drug trafficking, a major moneymaker endorsed by the mullahs through a particular fatwa. In addition to the production and trade of heroin in the Middle East, Hezbollah facilitates, for a fee, the trafficking for other drug-smuggling networks, such as the FARC and its cocaine trade."

Emanuele Ottolenghi   November 8, 2017

authorities, "since in or around 2006, such narcotics trafficking has been condoned through the issuance of fatwas by radical Islamic clerics."[30] Former U.S. officials familiar with Hezbollah drug trafficking cases told me, under condition of anonymity, that evidence seized in one instance included a written copy of a fatwa by a senior Hezbollah cleric endorsing the drug trade as a legitimate source of funding for the "resistance" – a code word for Hezbollah.[31]

In 2016, the Drug Enforcement Administration (DEA) identified a coherent, hierarchical structure inside Hezbollah that has been in charge of its illicit operations since as early as 2007. The DEA named it the BAC – an acronym for the Business Affairs Component of Hezbollah's External Security Organization – likely another name for the Islamic Jihad Organization. As stated in a February 2016 DEA press release:

> This global network, referred to by law enforcement as the Lebanese Hizballah External Security Organization Business Affairs Component (BAC), was founded by deceased Hizballah Senior Leader Imad Mughniyah and currently operates under the control of Abdallah Safieddine and recent U.S.-designated Specially Designated Global Terrorist (SDGT) Adham Tabaja. Members of the Hizballah BAC have established business relationships with South American drug cartels, such as La Oficina de Envigado, responsible for supplying large quantities of cocaine to the European and United States drug markets. Further, the Hizballah BAC continues to launder significant drug proceeds as part of a trade based money laundering scheme known as the Black Market Peso Exchange.[32]

Cases implicating the BAC give a sense of the global footprint of Hezbollah's illicit activities and offer a glimpse into the size of these operations. They also offer a blueprint for a strong and effective U.S. response to this threat.

In the first case, Treasury sanctioned the Tajideen brothers and their business network, operating mainly out of West Africa, in 2009[33] and then again in 2010.[34] In its initial designation, Treasury accused Kassem Tajideen of having contributed "tens of millions of dollars" to Hezbollah. Tajideen was eventually arrested in March 2017 in Morocco and extradited to the United States where he will stand trial. His initial indictment details $27 million in transactions with U.S.-based companies, where the corporate identity of Tajideen's business network was concealed.[35]

---

[30] Verified Amended Complaint, *United States of America v. Lebanese Canadian Bank SAL et al*, 11 Civ. 9186, (PAE), (SDNY filed October 26, 2012). (https://www.justice.gov/sites/default/files/usao-sdny/legacy/2015/03/25/U.S.%20v.%20Lebanese%20Canadian%20Bank%2C%20et%20al.%20Amended%20Complaint.pdf)

[31] Conversation with the author, October 24, 2017.

[32] United States Drug Enforcement Administration, Press Release, "DEA and European Authorities Uncover Massive Hizballah Drug and Money Laundering Scheme," February 1, 2016. (https://www.dea.gov/divisions/hq/2016/hq020116.shtml)

[33] U.S. Department of the Treasury, Press Release, "Treasury Targets Hizballah Financial Network," May 27, 2009. (https://www.treasury.gov/press-center/press-releases/Pages/tg149.aspx)

[34] U.S. Department of the Treasury, Press Release, "Treasury Targets Hizballah Financial Network," December 9, 2010. (https://www.treasury.gov/press-center/press-releases/Pages/tg997.aspx)

[35] Indictment, *United States of America v. Kassim Tajideen et al.*, No. 16-CV-64 (RBW) (D.D.C filed March 7, 2017). (https://www.justice.gov/opa/press-release/file/952071/download)

                                             November 8, 2017

In 2011, Treasury targeted the aforementioned Ayman Joumaa. According to Treasury, Joumaa and his network – which extended to South and Central America, West Africa, and Lebanon – laundered "as much as $200 million per month" in drug proceeds for Latin American drug cartels.[36] Joumaa was eventually indicted[37] but remains at large.

On February 1, 2016 the Drug Enforcement Administration announced multiple Hezbollah arrests in an operation involving seven countries.[38] The operation disrupted a ring responsible for moving large quantities of cocaine to the United States and Europe. According to a former U.S. official familiar with the case, the ring involved shipments of cocaine to Europe, which were paid for in Euros, and were then transferred to the Middle East by couriers. Hezbollah made more than €20 million a month selling its own cocaine in Europe. It also laundered tens of millions of Euros of cocaine proceeds on behalf of the cartels via the Black Market Peso Exchange, retaining a fee. During multiple arrests conducted across Europe, authorities seized €500,000 in cash, luxury watches worth $9 million that Hezbollah couriers intended to transport to the Middle East for sales at inflated prices, and property worth millions.[39] Money from drug sales was used to buy weapons for Hezbollah in Syria and to fund projects in Iraq run by Adham Tabaja – himself sanctioned in June 2015 for managing investment projects in Lebanon and Iraq on behalf of Hezbollah.[40]

In September 2016, the DEA indicted three Hezbollah members – one, Hassan Mohsen Mansour, was arrested in Paris – who were laundering cocaine proceeds for Colombian cartels. The charges against one of them, Mohammad Ammar, who was extradited to Miami, involved moving half a million dollars of drug money to U.S. banks in order to launder it, but the cash value of their operation was much larger.[41]

All these cases involved a sanctions and a law enforcement component. They also relied on unprecedented intelligence sharing and interagency coordination, cooperation with foreign law enforcement and intelligence agencies from allied countries, and the reliance on a panoply of tools drawn from the sanctions arsenal and the USA PATRIOT Act. The platform for this successful model was Project Cassandra, a decade-long operation run by the DEA through the Special Operations Division, a multi-agency coordination center that enables stakeholders from the law

---

[36] Jo Becker, "Beirut Bank Seen as a Hub of Hezbollah's Financing," *The New York Times,* December 13, 2011. (http://www.nytimes.com/2011/12/14/world/middleeast/beirut-bank-seen-as-a-hub-of-hezbollahs-financing.html). Joumaa's web of companies included U.S.-based businesses and the Canadian-Lebanese Bank. The combined force of U.S. sanctions, prosecutions, and financial restrictions on the bank eventually crippled Joumaa's network. Joumaa was indicted in December 2011 but remains at large.
[37] Indictment, *United States of America v. Ayman Joumaa,* No. 1:11-CR-560 (TSE), (EDVA November 23, 2011). (https://www.investigativeproject.org/documents/case_docs/1856.pdf)
[38] United States Drug Enforcement Administration, Press Release, "DEA and European Authorities Uncover Massive Hizballah Drug and Money Laundering Scheme," February 1, 2016. (https://www.dea.gov/divisions/hq/2016/hq020116.shtml)
[39] Information obtained from a former U.S. official familiar with the investigation. See also: David Asher, "Attacking Hezbollah's Financial Network: Policy Options," *Testimony before House Foreign Affairs Committee,* June 8, 2017. (http://docs.house.gov/meetings/FA/FA00/20170608/106094/HHRG-115-FA00-Wstate-AsherD-20170608.PDF)
[40] U.S. Department of the Treasury, Press Release, "Treasury Sanctions Hizballah Front Companies and Facilitators in Lebanon and Iraq," June 10, 2015. (https://www.treasury.gov/press-center/press-releases/Pages/jl0069.aspx)
[41] David Ovalle, "State: Hezbollah-linked group laundered drug money through Miami banks," *The Miami Herald,* October 11, 2016. (http://www.miamiherald.com/news/local/crime/article107366182.html)

                                        November 8, 2017

enforcement and intelligence community to share information and cooperate more effectively. This organizational model, and the outcomes it yielded through successful investigations, should be revived and resourced, moving forward, to ensure that U.S. success against Hezbollah operations is not merely tactical.[42]

Other suspected cases, if links to Hezbollah are confirmed, indicate how large the drug trafficking networks are in Latin America. In some cases, these networks intend to sell drugs inside the United States – a clear sign of how close to home the threat of Hezbollah's terror finance networks is.

In July 2016, Brazilian authorities arrested Fadi Hassan Nabha, a former Hezbollah Special Forces member wanted for drug trafficking. Brazil did not comment on his Hezbollah links, nor was he prosecuted under terrorism charges, since Brazil does not consider Hezbollah to be a terror group. Nevertheless, Nabha had a long history of drug trafficking – he was first arrested in 2003, in São Paulo, Brazil, in an operation where 42 kilos of cocaine were seized.[43] Media reports quoting police sources said at the time of the arrest Nabha's group was moving between 400 kilos and one ton of cocaine per month, which he and his associates bought, on the Brazilian side of the TBA, at $2,000 per kilo and sold in Brazil for $4,500 or in Lebanon for $60,000 – these are 2003 prices.[44]

In June 2017, U.S. authorities extradited Lebanese-Paraguayan national Ali Issa Chamas to Miami on charges of conspiring to ship cocaine to the United States. At the time of his arrest in Paraguay, Chamas was dispatching a shipment of 39 kilograms of cocaine to Turkey from the Guarani International Airport outside Ciudad Del Este in the TBA. Court documents[45] show that Chamas was part of a larger network of drug traffickers, likely based in Colombia. Had he not been arrested, Chamas would have dispatched a test run of three kilos of cocaine to a business partner in Houston. Upon successful receipt of the test run, Chamas promised his partner as many as 100 kilos of cocaine a month could be shipped, by air cargo, to the U.S. He noted that "it would take 4 to 5 days to Houston, 2 to 3 days to Miami, 4 days to Toronto, Canada" and indicated that air cargo was the method of transport.[46]

Chamas' arrest eventually led to the detention, by Paraguayan authorities, of three of his associates. On February 4, 2017 two Turkish nationals were detained in their TBA apartment.[47] There, police found a press, believed to serve the purpose of liquefying cocaine, and 65 large shampoo bottles,

---

[42] A detailed description of Project Cassandra and its achievement can be found in: Derek Maltz, "Attacking Hezbollah's Financial Network: Policy Options," *Testimony before House Foreign Affairs Committee*, June 8, 2017. (http://docs.house.gov/meetings/FA/FA00/20170608/106094/HHRG-115-FA00-Wstate-MaltzD-20170608.pdf)

[43] "Polícia prende dois libaneses com 42 quilos de cocaína (Police apprehend two Lebanese with 42 kilos of Cocaine)," *Folha de S. Paulo* (Brazil), January 23, 2003.
(http://www1.folha.uol.com.br/folha/cotidiano/ult95u67289.shtml)

[44] "Denarc appreende cocaína de máfia libanesa (Denarc apprehend cocaine of Lebanese mafia)," *Agencia Estado* (Brazil), January 23, 2003. (http://brasil.estadao.com.br/noticias/geral,denarc-apreende-cocaina-da-mafia-libanesa,20030123p4658)

[45] United States of America's Factual Proffer for Defendant's Change of Plea, *United States of America v. Ali Issa Chamas*, No. 16-20913-Williams (November 24, 2017). (https://ecf.flsd.uscourts.gov/doc1/051118408644)

[46] United States of America's Factual Proffer for Defendant's Change of Plea, *United States of America v. Ali Issa Chamas*, No. 16-20913-Williams (November 24, 2017). (https://ecf.flsd.uscourts.gov/doc1/051118408644)

[47] "Senad detiene a dos turcos con cocaína líquida en CDE" (Senad arrests two Turkish nationls with liquid cocaine in Ciudad Del Este)," *Ultima Hora* (Paraguay), February 6, 2017. (http://www.ultimahora.com/senad-detiene-dos-turcos-cocaina-liquida-cde-n1060868.html).

Emanuele Ottolenghi

which investigators believe were meant to be used to carry the drugs.[48] One of the two individuals arrested had photographs of cocaine powder and packaged cocaine in his mobile phone. On April 6, 2017, a fourth individual, also a Lebanese national, was detained in his Ciudad Del Este apartment, while in the company of two others. Media and police reports independently obtained from local sources indicate that Chamas and his associates are suspected of being part of the same trafficking network and to have ties to Hezbollah.[49]

Hezbollah may also have been linked to Latin American drug baron Rafaat Jorge Toumani, a Brazilian national of Syrian descent who was gunned down in the Paraguay-Brazil frontier town of Pedro Juan Caballero in June 2016.[50] Toumani, at the time, was involved in a $30-million real estate project with Lebanese partners suspected of links with Hezbollah.[51] The real estate project – a large commercial mall on the border of Paraguay and Brazil – was likely a money-laundering scheme for drug proceeds and floundered once Toumani was assassinated.

Toumani was considered the heir to Fahd Jamil-Georges,[52] a Lebanese-Brazilian drug lord who controlled much of the Paraguay-Brazil drug transportation land route and whom the United States designated in 2006 under the Kingpin Act.[53] The U.S. government considered Jamil-Georges, alongside four other Lebanese clans well rooted in the Brazil-Paraguay border towns, to be "the major actors in drugs and other large-scale crimes;"[54] the other four families have well-established links to Hezbollah. Despite his Kingpin designation dating back to 2006, Jamil-Georges remains at large and is rumored to live just across the Brazilian border, inside Paraguay, in the city where Toumani was gunned down. Local sources allege that he lives off proceeds from a large local real estate development.

Chamas was in charge of shipping hundreds of kilos of cocaine a month. His associates were also handling significant quantities of cocaine. Toumani was also handling billions worth of cocaine

---

[48] "Caen dos narcotraficantes turcos (Turkish narcotraffickers arrested)," *ABC Color* (Paraguay), February 6, 2017. (http://www.abc.com.py/edicion-impresa/judiciales-y-policiales/caen-dos-narcotraficantes-turcos-1562260.html)
[49] For more details, see my May 2017 Testimony: Emanuele Ottolenghi, "Emerging External Influences in the Western Hemisphere," *Testimony before Senate Foreign Relations Committee*, May 10, 2017. (https://www.foreign.senate.gov/imo/media/doc/051017_Ottolenghi_Testimony.pdf); See also: "Extraditarán a Libaés por partenecer al grupo terrorista Hezbollah." *Paraguay Noticias*, May 19, 2017. (http://www.paraguay.com/nacionales/extraditaran-a-libanes-por-pertenecer-al-grupo-terrorista-hezbollah-162907); Jay Weaver, "Paraguayan man linked to Hezbollah faces drug charges in Miami," *The Miami Herald*, June 26, 2017. (http://www.miamiherald.com/news/local/crime/article158334659.html)
[50] David Gagne, "Killing of Mysterious Figure Part of Larger Narco War in Paraguay?" *Insight Crime*, June 16, 2016. (http://www.insightcrime.org/news-briefs/killing-of-mysterious-figure-part-of-paraguay-narco-war)
[51] "A pesar de pocas ventas, grupo empresarial construye moderno shopping center en Pedro Juan (Under weight of low sales, business group contructs modern shopping center in Pedro Juan)," *Amambay Digital* (Paraguay), March 23, 2013. (https://www.amambaydigital.com/id-660-cat-1-uri-a-pesar-de-pocas-ventas-grupo-empresarial-construye-moderno-shopping-center-en-pedro-juan.html)
[52] "Confiscan 847 kilos de cocaína del capomafioso fronterizo Jorge Rafat (847 kilos of cocaine confiscated from frontier mafia head Jorge Rafaat)," *ABC Color* (Paraguay), August 22, 2014. (http://www.abc.com.py/edicion-impresa/judiciales-y-policiales/confiscan-847-kilos-de-cocaina-del-capomafioso-fronterizo-jorge-rafat-1278422.html)
[53] U.S. Department of the Treasury, "Recent OFAC Actions," June 1, 2006. (https://www.treasury.gov/resource-center/sanctions/OFAC-Enforcement/Pages/20060601.aspx)
[54] "Interagency Cooperation on Tri-Border Area," *Wikileaks Cable: 07ASUNCION688 a*, August 20, 2007. (https://wikileaks.org/plusd/cables/07ASUNCION688_a.html)

Emanuele Ottolenghi   November 8, 2017

transactions. Assuming links to Hezbollah can be confirmed in all these cases, this is another piece of the puzzle that is Hezbollah's multi-billion dollar drug and money-laundering empire in Latin America.

Mr. Chairman, combating this growing risk to the American homeland needs to be a U.S. policy priority, especially when one considers the scale of Hezbollah's revenues from its global involvement in criminal activities. A September 2017 assessment of Hezbollah finances published by two of my colleagues concluded that Hezbollah's overseas financial networks' contributions to its budget have mushroomed to an estimated 20-30 percent of their overall operating budget, which my colleagues conservatively estimated to be around $1 billion a year.[55]

An exact figure is hard to come by without access to classified information and knowledge of ongoing investigations. Regardless, it is fair to conclude that proceeds from criminal activities have become a vital source of income for Hezbollah, especially when one looks at available evidence. The cases the U.S. prosecuted in recent years as part of Project Cassandra reveal that Hezbollah was implicated in laundering billions of drug money and moving large quantities of drugs globally.

America needs to recognize the magnitude and scale of this problem and dedicate its best resources to fighting it. This is a direct threat to the homeland and all tools need to be leveraged in a combined fashion to yield the desired results.

Mr. Chairman, I have discussed the nature and magnitude of the threat of Hezbollah in Latin America. This panel seeks to determine whether the Kingpin Act is being effective in the Western Hemisphere. In Latin America, Hezbollah has certainly benefited from the lack of U.S. enforcement of its own sanctions coupled with a permissive environment where corrupt local officials connive with Hezbollah's illicit finance schemes for their own personal gain.

Actions taken by the U.S. to update and enforce its own existing sanctions against Hezbollah terror-finance networks would be a first step to reverse this situation. That would naturally have to include Kingpin designations. But much more is needed.

HEZBOLLAH'S IMPUNITY IN LATIN AMERICA: THE CASE OF UNENFORCED U.S. SANCTIONS

Starting in 2004, the U.S. Department of the Treasury periodically sanctioned Hezbollah-linked individuals and entities in the TBA.[56] Treasury cited their involvement in raising funds for Hezbollah, often through illicit finance and trade activities, as a key reason for sanctions. To date, the U.S. has only sanctioned 11 individuals and 4 companies in the TBA for their involvement with Hezbollah's terror-finance networks. Despite recognizing the importance of the TBA for

[55] Yaya J. Fanusie and Alex Entz, "Hezbollah Financial Assessment," *Foundation for Defense of Democracies*, September 2017. (http://www.defenddemocracy.org/content/uploads/documents/CSIF_TFBB_Hezbollah.pdf)
[56] U.S. Department of the Treasury, Press Release, "Treasury Targets Hizballah Fundraising Network in the Triple Frontier of Argentina, Brazil, and Paraguay," December 6, 2006. (https://www.treasury.gov/press-center/press-releases/Pagés/hp190.aspx); U.S. Department of the Treasury, Press Release, "Treasury Targets Hizballah Financial Network," December 9, 2010. (https://www.treasury.gov/press-center/press-releases/Pagés/tg997.aspx)

Hezbollah's terror finance in 2004, the U.S. government has not leveraged U.S. sanctions and designations as effectively and aggressively as it could and has not gone after additional members of the Hezbollah TBA networks. For over a decade since designations occurred, the TBA has only seen one law enforcement case, in 2010, when U.S.-based businesses were caught shipping merchandise to these sanctioned entities and faced prosecution, convictions, and fines.

If anything, the area remains an important center of Hezbollah's activities, as I have previously documented in a June 2016 testimony to the House Financial Services Committee[57] and a May 2017 testimony to the Senate Foreign Relations Committee.[58] Evidence of its importance emerges from multiple reports from local sources of the arrival of senior Hezbollah operatives in the area since 2016[59] and the recent death of Samer Ibrahim Atoui,[60] a senior Hezbollah commander. Atoui may well have been a member of Hezbollah's BAC. Though he died in Eastern Syria while driving with another senior Hezbollah Special Forces commander,[61] thousands of miles away from Latin America, Atoui held both Brazilian and Paraguayan citizenships.

> [illegible]
> 08505.003541/98-99);
> SAMER IBRAHIM ATOUI - Y000349, natural do Líbano, nascido em 8 de janeiro de 1969, filho de Ibrahim Atoui e de Ayda Nehme, residente no Estado de São Paulo (Processo nº PC 08505.003553/98-78) ; e

Extract from Brazil's official records showing Samer Ibrahim Atoui's naturalization in 1998

---

[57] Emanuele Ottolenghi, "The Enemy in our Backyard: Examining Terror Funding Streams from South America." *Testimony before House Committee on Financial Services*, June 8, 2016.
(http://www.defenddemocracy.org/content/uploads/documents/Ottolenghi_The_Enemy_in_our_Backyard.pdf)
[58] Emanuele Ottolenghi, "The Enemy in our Backyard: Examining Terror Funding Streams from South America." *Testimony before House Committee on Financial Services*, June 8, 2016.
(http://www.defenddemocracy.org/content/uploads/documents/Ottolenghi_The_Enemy_in_our_Backyard.pdf)
[59] Conversation with the author, May 5. 2017.
[60] Ziad El Shoufi, "بالصور : الخيام تودع القائد الشهيد سامر ابراهيم عطوي" (Pictures: Khayyam deposed martyr Samer Ibrahim Atwi)," *Khiam Village Official Pagé*, October 5, 2017.
(http://www.khiyam.com/news/article.php?articleID=25298)
[61] Qalaat Al Mudiq, *Twitter*, October 2, 2017, accessed November 1. 2017.
(https://twitter.com/QalaatAlMudiq/status/914821544362332160); Social media initially identified Atoui with his nom de guerre Abu Ali Jawad.

Emanuele Ottolenghi

November 8, 2017

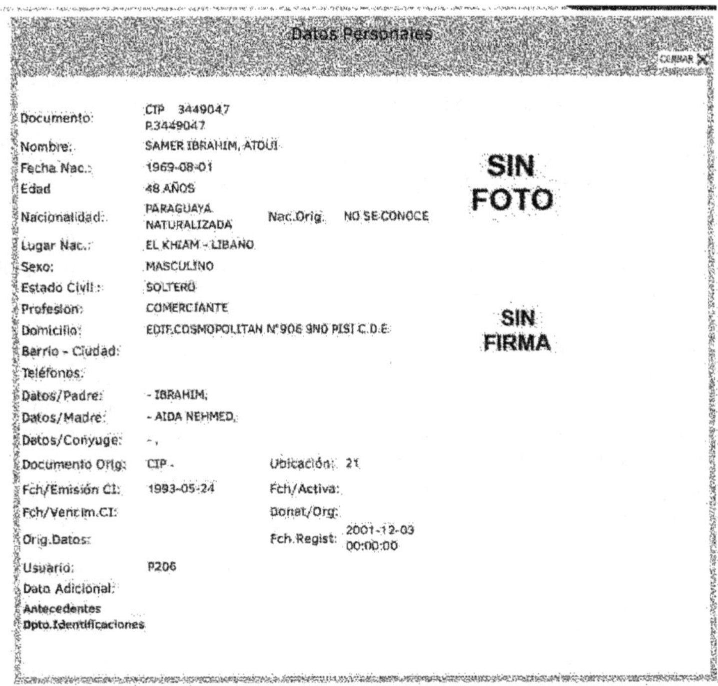

Official Record of Samer Ibrahim Atoui in Paraguay, showing his Identity Card was issued in 1993, five years before he was granted Brazilian citizenship

Based on public records of his dual citizenship, we assess that Atoui spent at least five years in the TBA during the early 1990s. Based on evidence available on social media, including the fact that the Imam Khomeini mosque in Foz do Iguazu, on the Brazilian side of the TBA, commemorated him four days after his death,[62] we also assess that he had close family ties in Latin America and maintained close relations with Hezbollah TBA Specially Designated Global Terrorists (SDGT) and other prominent members of the TBA-based Hezbollah network.[63]

These ties suggest that the TBA remains a high priority for Hezbollah's funding operations. U.S. sanctions clearly failed to deter Hezbollah in the TBA. In fact, evidence of people who have previously been identified as senior Hezbollah operatives focusing on the TBA and, even more so, relocating there permanently, suggests that the opposite is true.

---

[62] Mohamad Moha Ali, *Facebook*, October 6, 2017, accessed November 1, 2017. (https://www.facebook.com/photo.php?fbid=227982131067500&set=ecnf.100015671443264&type=3&theater)
[63] Bassam Nader, *Facebook*, October 2, 2017, accessed November 1, 2017. (https://www.facebook.com/photo.php?fbid=1711394692227524&set=a.561711337195871.1073741825.100000710303599&type=3&theater)

Emanuele Ottolenghi   November 8, 2017

As a result of Treasury's actions, sanctioned individuals and their businesses should have been cut off from the U.S. financial system. Since November 2015, Congressional legislation targeting Hezbollah's global financial networks should also have made them the object of secondary sanctions, extending penalties to those providing them material support. Evidence available from open sources, particularly social media, suggests that despite U.S. measures, many sanctioned Hezbollah operatives remain active in trade and finance, are able to travel abroad, and must therefore enjoy significant access to the global financial system.

Lack of enforcement is not because the TBA is no longer important to Hezbollah's terror finance. According to the June 2017 Department of State's Bureau of Counterterrorism and Countering Violent Extremism's Country Reports on Terrorism 2016:

> The Tri-Border Area continued to be attractive to individuals seeking to engage in terrorist financing, as the minimal police and military presence along these borders allowed for a largely unregulated flow of people, licit and illicit goods, and money. Paraguay's efforts to provide more effective law enforcement and border security were hampered by a lack of interagency cooperation and information sharing, as well as pervasive corruption within security, border control, and judicial institutions.[64]

The U.S. can and should seek to prevent SDGTs under E.O. 13224 from accessing the global financial system and punish those who offer them material support. Local circumstances at least partially explain the failure of U.S. sanctions to affect these individuals and entities.

As the March 2017 Department of State's International Narcotics Control Strategy Report explains:

> Paraguay is a drug transit country and money laundering center. The Tri-Border Area … is home to a multi-billion dollar contraband trade that facilitates much of the money laundering in Paraguay. Transnational criminal organizations operating in these three countries are believed to launder the proceeds from narcotics trafficking and other illicit activities through banks and non-bank financial sector entities. Paraguay's progress in combating money laundering is impeded by widespread corruption, burdensome bureaucracy, and the fear of reprisal against regulatory and supervisory authorities.[65]

The counterterrorism Country Report on Paraguay for 2016 also highlights inadequate enforcement. In the Paraguay section, the report states that "Paraguay has counterterrorist financing legislation and the ability to freeze without delay and confiscate terrorist assets, although there were no terrorist financing convictions or actions to freeze in 2016."[66]

---

[64] U.S Department of State, "Chapter 2. Country Reports: Western Hemisphere," *Country Reports on Terrorism 2016*, July 2017. (https://www.state.gov/j/ct/rls/crt/2016/272234.htm)

[65] U.S. Department of State, Bureau for International Narcotics and Law Enforcement Affairs, "International Narcotics Control Strategy Report: Volume II: Money Laundering and Financial Crimes," March 2017. (https://www.state.gov/documents/organization/268024.pdf)

[66] U.S Department of State, "Chapter 2. Country Reports: Western Hemisphere," *Country Reports on Terrorism 2016*, July 2017. (https://www.state.gov/j/ct/rls/crt/2016/272234.htm)

Emanuele Ottolenghi

November 8, 2017

All sanctioned Hezbollah operatives to date operate from the TBA, run Paraguay-registered businesses, and hold Paraguayan citizenship. Many reside in Brazil. Some hold dual nationality or permanent residency in both countries. Their ability to move freely between these two jurisdictions is a testimony to the ineffectiveness of U.S. measures when not matched by local authorities' cooperation. The following evidence for six individuals and one entity under U.S. sanctions makes it abundantly clear that, as a result of this permissive environment, SDGTs can shrug off the effects of U.S. Treasury designations.

I.   Sobhi Mahmoud Fayad

Sobhi Mahmoud Fayad was designated by the U.S. Treasury Department in 2006 for serving as a liaison with the Iranian embassy on behalf of the Hezbollah community in the TBA. According to Treasury, he was involved in drug trafficking and in counterfeiting U.S. currency. He was also sentenced to six and a half years of prison in Paraguay for tax evasion.[67]

Despite U.S. sanctions and a Paraguayan prison sentence (which he served in full), evidence posted by Fayad himself on his Facebook account provides abundant evidence of his travels and activities. His extensive travel also suggests he retains access to financial tools to pay for his needs – an indication that local banks are unlikely to be enforcing U.S. sanctions against him.[68]

In a September 2016 trip to fulfill the Islamic pilgrimage obligation, or the *Haji*, in Saudi Arabia, for example, Fayad flew from Foz do Iguaçu to São Paulo, Brazil, where he boarded an Ethiopian airlines flight to Addis Ababa (via Togo). From Addis Ababa he connected to Beirut, where he spent at least a day,[69] before joining a group of Lebanese pilgrims heading to Saudi Arabia. While in Saudi Arabia, he posted information regarding his whereabouts, including the hotel where he was staying.[70] Upon completion of the *Haji*, Fayad returned to Lebanon and then, eventually, the TBA.

---

[67] U.S. Department of the Treasury, Press Release, "Treasury Targets Hezbollah Fundraising Network in the Triple Frontier of Argentina, Brazil and Paraguay," December 6, 2006. (https://www.treasury.gov/press-center/press-releases/Pagés/hp190.aspx)

[68] According to §566.601 of the Department of the Treasury's Hezbollah Financial Sanctions regulations issued in April 2016: "(a) A foreign financial institution engages in an activity described in this paragraph if, in any location or currency, the foreign financial institution, on or after December 18, 2015, knowingly: (1) Facilitates a significant transaction or transactions for Hizballah; (2) Facilitates a significant transaction or transactions of a person identified on OFAC's Specially Designated Nationals and Blocked Persons List (SDN List), the property and interests in property of which are blocked pursuant to the International Emergency Economic Powers Act (50 U.S.C. 1701 *et seq.*) (IEEPA) for acting on behalf of or at the direction of, or being owned or controlled by, Hizballah." Hizballah Financial Sanctions Regulations, 31 e-C.F.R. §566.601, November 2, 2017. (https://www.ecfr.gov/cgi-bin/text-idx?SID=235c0575169c66186fc81c00ccaf83fc&mc=true&node=pt31.3.566&rgn=div5#se31.3.566_1202).

[69] Sobhi Fayad, *Facebook*, August 30, 2016. (https://www.facebook.com/sobhif1/posts/1181410128548341?pnref=story).

[70] Sobhi Fayad, *Facebook*, September 3, 2016. (https://www.facebook.com/sobhif1/posts/1184034418285912?pnref=story)

Emanuele Ottolenghi   November 8, 2017

He returned to Saudi Arabia this year,[71] flying from Rio de Janeiro to Beirut, Lebanon before landing in Mecca.[72] He also recently visited Damascus.[73]

Fayad appears to be traveling on a valid Paraguayan passport, which he posted on his Facebook account[74] to show a visa to Iraq, in December 2015, when he went to Karbala on pilgrimage. According to information Fayad posted on the same day,[75] he bought a ticket on an Iraqi Airways flight to Najaf from Beirut from the airline's Beirut office and paid in dollars.

These details are important because Treasury identified Fayad as a Hezbollah operative in the TBA. According to the 2004 Treasury designation of Fayad's boss, Assaad Ahmad Barakat, Fayad at the time was a known Hezbollah senior operative and weapons and explosives expert. According to Treasury,[76] Fayad, "a high-ranking Hizballah official in Lebanon in the 1980s," supported Hezbollah operations in the TBA. In its subsequent 2006 designation of Fayad, Treasury noted his regular trips to Lebanon and Iran to coordinate with Hezbollah leaders.[77]

II.   Bilal Mohsen Wehbe

Bilal Mohsen Wehbe was sanctioned in 2010 for being Hezbollah's "chief representative in South America."[78] He is one of the leading sheiks in Brazil's Centro Islamico do Brasil (Islamic Center of Brazil) and regularly participates in prayers, educational events,[79] and meetings. In 2015, he was photographed at a public meeting with Hassan Khomeini, the grandson of Islamic Republic of Iran's founder Ayatollah Khomeini, on his trip to Brazil and Paraguay alongside various other

---

[71] Sobhi Fayad, *Facebook*, August 30, 2017.
(https://www.facebook.com/photo.php?fbid=1532357460120271&set=pb.100000380942311.-2207520000.1506524710.&type=3&theater); Sobhi Fayad, *Facebook*, August 30, 2017.
(https://www.facebook.com/sobhif1/videos/pcb.1532358160120201/1532357590120258/?type=3&theater); Sobhi Fayad, *Facebook*, August 29, 2017. (https://www.facebook.com/sobhif1/posts/1531901153499235)
[72] Sobhi Fayad, *Facebook*, August 27, 2017. (https://www.facebook.com/sobhif1/posts/1529471460408871); Sobhi Fayad, *Facebook*, August 27, 2017. (https://www.facebook.com/sobhif1/posts/1529471297075554); Sobhi Fayad, *Facebook*, August 22, 2017. (https://www.facebook.com/sobhif1/posts/1525799624109388)
[73] Sobhi Fayad, *Facebook*, October 29, 2017.
(https://www.facebook.com/photo.php?fbid=1584461478243202&set=pb.100000380942311.-2207520000.1509638511.&type=3&theater)
[74] Sobhi Fayad, *Facebook*, November 28, 2015.
(https://www.facebook.com/photo.php?fbid=10153351825154173&set=pb.100000380942311.-2207520000.1474041934.&type=3&theater)
[75] Sobhi Fayad, *Facebook*, November 24, 2015.
(https://www.facebook.com/photo.php?fbid=10154428084784408&set=pb.100000380942311.-2207520000.1493994894.&type=3&size=960%2C720)
[76] U.S Department of the Treasury, Press Release, "Treasury Designated Islamic Extremist, Two Companies Supporting Hizballah in Tri-Border Area," June 10, 2004. (https://www.treasury.gov/press-center/press-releases/Pages/js1720.aspx)
[77] U.S. Department of the Treasury, Press Release, "Treasury Targets Hizballah Fundraising Network in the Triple Frontier of Argentina, Brazil and Paraguay," December 6, 2006. (https://www.treasury.gov/press-center/press-releases/Pages/hp190.aspx)
[78] U.S Department of the Treasury, Press Release, "Treasury Targets Hizballah Financial Network," December 9, 2010. (https://www.treasury.gov/press-center/press-releases/Pages/tg997.aspx)
[79] Lecture at the Brazilian Association of Islamic Charity, Bilal Wehbe, *Facebook*, May 2, 2017.
(https://www.facebook.com/100001550997469/videos/vb.100001550997469/1423895684338784/?type=2&theater)

Emanuele Ottolenghi   November 8, 2017

TBA religious and political figures.[80] In February 2017, he welcomed the Iraqi ambassador to Brazil, H.E. Mr. Arshad Omar Esmaeel, to Arresala,[81] an Islamic cultural center based in São Paulo. Wehbe continues to operate in Brazil, where authorities have not interfered with his activities.

III.   Hatem Barakat

Treasury sanctioned Hatem Barakat and two other family members in 2006.[82] Nevertheless, he appears to remain active in business. Hatem lists his current employment at a store named Infornet Princesa.[83] The store is located in Luanda, Angola and sells electronics, children's toys, and accessories.[84]

IV.   Hamze Ahmad Barakat

Hamze Ahmad Barakat was arrested in Curitiba, Brazil in May 2013 for operating a "fraudulent scheme in the clothing industry" after his 2006 designation by the U.S. Treasury for his membership with, and financing of, Hezbollah.[85] According to social media evidence, Hamze appears to continue to operate businesses in the Brazilian clothing industry.[86] The store that was originally designated along with him and his brother since 2006, Casa Hamze, appears to no longer exist. Commercial registry entries show that Hamze Barakat is listed as the owner and/or

---

[80] Bilal Wehbe, *Facebook*, March 23, 2015.
(https://www.facebook.com/photo.php?fbid=871182302943461&set=pb.100001550997469.-2207520000.1473430163.&type=3&theater); Arresala, *Flickr*, "Sua Eminencia Seyyed Hassan Khomeini no Centro Islamico no Brasil Junho/2015 (Our Eminence Seyyed Hassan Khomeini at Islamic Center of Brazil on June 2015)." (https://www.flickr.com/photos/arresala/albums/72157654222225772)

[81] Arresala – Centro Islamico do Brasil, *Flickr*, February 3, 2017.
(https://www.flickr.com/photos/arresala/3274507624 5/in/photostream/)

[82] Department of the Treasury, Press Release. "Treasury Targets Hezbollah Fundraising Network in the Triple Frontier of Argentina, Brazil, and Paraguay," December 6, 2006. (https://www.treasury.gov/press-center/press-releases/Pages/hp190.aspx)

[83] Hatem Barakat, *Facebook*. accessed November 1, 2017.
(https://www.facebook.com/profile.php?id=100008314491434&sk=about)

[84] Infornet Princesa, *Facebook*, March 13, 2013.
(https://www.facebook.com/InfornetPrincesa/photos/a.148099262011675.33296.147243702097231/1629260405289 97/?type=3&theater); Infornet Princesa, *Facebook*, January 30, 2013.
(https://www.facebook.com/InfornetPrincesa/photos/a.148099262011675.33296.147243702097231/1494521985430 48/?type=3&theater); Infornet Princesa, *Facebook*, January 28, 2013.
(https://www.facebook.com/InfornetPrincesa/photos/a.147997282021873.33264.147243702097231/1479972853552 06/?type=1&theater)

[85] Simon Romero, "Businessman Linked by U.S. To Hezbollah is Arrested in Brazil in a Fraud Scheme," *The New York Times*, May 20, 2013. (http://www.nytimes.com/2013/05/21/world/americas/man-linked-by-us-to-hezbollah-is-arrested-in-brazil.html?_r=0)

[86] Hamze Ahmad Barakat, *Facebook*, accessed September 13, 2016.
(https://www.facebook.com/goldshoescalcadosxy); Hamze Barakat, *Facebook*, accessed September 13, 2016.
(https://www.facebook.com/profile.php?id=100003744833939); Hamze Barakat, *Facebook*, September 13, 2016.
(https://www.facebook.com/profile.php?id=100004543359651); Hamze Barakat, *Facebook*. accessed September 13, 2016; (https://www.facebook.com/hamze.barakat.779); Hamze Barakat, *Facebook*, accessed September 13, 2016.
(https://www.facebook.com/hamze.barakat.77)

Emanuele Ottolenghi   November 8, 2017

administrator of at least four other businesses: Habhab & Barakat LTDA,[87] Minimundo Comercio de Artigos do Vestuario Ltda – ME d.b.a. Minimundo Importacao e Exportacao,[88] H.H Yassine & Cia Ltda,[89] and M V de Almeida e Cia Ltda d.b.a. Gold Shoes.[90]

V.   Mohammad Tarabain Chamas

Sanctioned in 2006 with the Barakat brothers, Mohammad Tarabain Chamas was named by Treasury as the administrator of Galeria Pagé.[91] He was also named as proprietor and vice president of Hi-Tech Digital Technology S.A. in 2005. It is unclear whether the business is still active.[92] As of 2011, Tarabain Chamas has been running a parking garage in Foz de Iguaçu named Cars Estacionamento.[93] According to a local source, Tarabain Chamas has also moved to Galeria Conquistador, a shopping mall in Ciudad Del Este adjacent to Galeria Pagé, where he has been appointed administrator.[94]

Business card of Mohammad Tarabain listed as administrator of Galeria Conquistador from June 2016 with Kemel Tarabain.[95]

---

[87] "Habhab & Barakat Ltda," *Sales Spider*, accessed September 19, 2016. (http://www.salespider.com/bw-12669317/habhab-barakat-ltda)

[88] "Hamze Ahmad Barakat," *ConsultaSocio.com* (Brazil), accessed September 19, 2016. (http://www.consultasocio.com/q/sa/hamze-ahmad-barakat)

[89] "H.H. Yassine & Cia Ltda," *Diretorio da Empresas Econodata*, accessed November 6, 2017. (http://www.econodata.com.br/lista-empresas/PARANA/CURITIBA/H/05559600000108-H-H-YASSINE-CIA-LTDA-EPP)

[90] "Gold Shoes," *CPNJ Brasil*, accessed September 19, 2016. (http://www.cnpjbrasil.com/e/cnpj/gold-shoes/09391146000180)

[91] U.S. Department of the Treasury, Press Release, "Treasury Targets Hizballah Fundraising Network in the Triple Fronteir of Argentina, Brazil and Paraguay," December 6, 2006. (https://www.treasury.gov/press-center/press-releases/Pagés/hp190.aspx)

[92] Paraguay Gabinete Civil de la Presidencia, "Gaceta Oficial de la República del Paraguay (Official Gazette of the Republic of Paraguay)," February 23, 2006. (http://www.gacetaoficial.gov.pv/uploads/pdf/2014/2014-02-14/gaceta_2240_HIEGDIIAEBKGKKHBIDAFFJAFCIGHGGKCDDJHBGIF.pdf) The PDF has been removed from Paraguay's Official Gazette. FDD has a copy, which is available upon request.

[93] "Cars Estacionamento | Mohamed Tarabain Chamas – Me," *CPNJ Info* (Brazil), accessed September 15, 2016. (http://cupj.info/CARS-ESTACIONAMENTO-MOHAMED-TARABAIN-CHAMAS-ME-Tr-Julio-Pasa-74-Foz-Do-Iguacu-PR-85851370/aLiC/)

[94] Emanuele Ottolenghi, "What Netanyahu should ask Paraguay's president," *The Jerusalem Post* (Israel), July 17, 2016. (http://www.jpost.com/Opinion/The-question-Netanyahu-should-raise-to-visiting-president-of-Paraguay-460664)

[95] Image was received from confidential source.

Emanuele Ottolenghi   November 8, 2017

VI.   Mohammad Fayez Barakat

Mohammad Fayez Barakat was also sanctioned in 2006 for his involvement in moving funds to Hezbollah from the TBA.[96] Since then, he has remained a prominent and influential figure in the Lebanese community of Paraguay. According to official Paraguay records, he continues to own Big Boss International Import Export, a store located inside the U.S.-sanctioned Galeria Pagé.[97]

Mohammad Fayez Barakat, attending the November 2016 Embassy of Lebanon Independence Day reception in Asuncion, Paraguay.[98]

---

[96] U.S. Department of the Treasury, Press Release, "Treasury targets Hizballah Fundraising Network in the Triple Fronteir of Argentina, Brazil and Paraguay," December 6, 2006. (https://www.treasury.gov/press-center/press-releases/Pagés/hp190.aspx)

[97] Paraguay official records.

[98] Photo obtained from a local source.

In 2014, Barakat was interviewed as a witness of the brutal beating of an individual in the Galeria Pagé, where his store "Big Boss" is located.[99] Big Boss International Import Export stands accused of suspicious activity, including in 2008, when Mohamad Fayez and his brother Ali Fayez were investigated for allegedly transferring $88,480 through Banco Amambay in 2005 and 2006.[100] Nonetheless, Barakat remains active in Paraguay and so does his business.

VII. *Galeria Pagé aka Galeria Uniamerica*

The Ciudad Del Este shopping mall, Galeria Pagé was sanctioned in 2006 as a source of funding for Hezbollah-linked activities. Renamed as Shopping Uniamérica, the mall, which is still under U.S. sanctions, continues to operate today.[101] Shopping Uniamérica hosts stores and offices owned by Lebanese merchants, some of whom are themselves under U.S. sanctions due to their affiliation with Hezbollah in the TBA. Due to U.S. sanctions against the mall, all its shops are automatically blocked from doing business with U.S. persons and corporate entities. If proven to be transacting with and offering material support to Galeria Pagé, they are also liable to secondary U.S. sanctions.

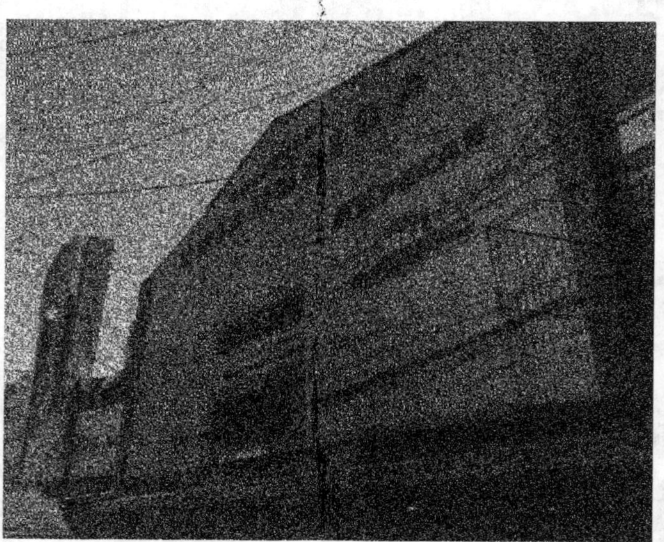

[99] "Fiscalía pedirá peritaje de filmación de brutal golpiza en Ciudad Del Este (Prosecutor's Office will request expert assessment of the video showing brutal beating in Ciudad Del Este)," *ABC Color* (Paraguay), June 3, 2014. (http://www.abc.com.py/edicion-impresa/judiciales-y-policiales/fiscalia-pedira-peritaje-de-filmacion-de-brutal-golpiza-en-ciudad-del-este-1251430.html)

[100] "Seprelad confirma 'operaciones sospechosas' de empresario libanes (Seprelad confirms 'suspicious operations' of Lebanese businessman)." *ABC Color* (Paraguay), November 30, 2008. (http://www.abc.com.py/edicion-impresa/policiales/seprelad-confirma-operaciones-sospechosas-de-empresario-libanes-1125542.html)

[101] "Lista de precos: Totas as Lojas – produto = gal Pagé – tipo todos (List of prices: All Stores – product = gal Pagé – type: all)," *Compras no Paraguai* (Brazil), accessed November 2, 2017. (http://www.comprasnoparaguai.com/precos.php?wcat=gal+Pagé); U.S. Department of the Treasury, Press Release, "Treasury Targets Hizballah Fundraising Network in the Triple Frontier of Argentina, Brazil and Paraguay," December 6, 2006. (https://www.treasury.gov/press-center/press-releases/Pagés/hp190.aspx)

Emanuele Ottolenghi

November 8, 2017

Through research conducted jointly with Sayari Analytics, FDD was able to identify 66 businesses and shops inside Galeria Pagé. Of these 66, we could only find official records proving their presence in or association with the Galeria for nine of them. Some of the records, however, are old and while they prove these companies were located in the Galeria after it was sanctioned, they do not always constitute conclusive evidence that they are still located there.

We also found six companies which, on their websites or Facebook pages, listed Galeria Pagé as their address.

There is a significant discrepancy between the numbers of actual businesses advertised inside the Galeria on commercial platforms, through their Facebook pages, on their website, and the ones identifiable through up-to-date tax records, official gazette entries, and trademark registrations. And as indicated, some entries appear to have been deleted or are blocked to viewers.

Screenshot of cancelled entry for Sobhi Mahmoud Fayad[102]

According to a Paraguayan official speaking to us on the condition of anonymity, the absence of businesses from the public registry of Paraguay's ministry of industry is deliberately made inaccessible through bribes.[103] It is impossible to independently verify this allegation.

This obfuscation attempt, if true, violates U.S. law and is liable to penalties under U.S. Treasury's Hezbollah financial regulations.[104]

---

[102] Paraguay official records.

[103] Conversation with the author, October 31, 2017.

[104] U.S. Department of the Treasury's Hizballah Financial Regulations' section 566.602 state that "(a) Any transaction on or after the effective date that evades or avoids, has the purpose of evading or avoiding, causes a violation of, or attempts to violate any of the prohibitions set forth in this part is prohibited. (b) Any conspiracy

Emanuele Ottolenghi   November 8, 2017

The evidence shown indicates that unless U.S. sanctions are followed by constant update and vigorous enforcement, targeted individuals and entities can soon elude them and shrug off their effects, especially if they can count on local corrupt authorities to collude with them. It is important that U.S. action be undertaken to rectify this state of affairs for two reasons. SDGTs may continue to engage in nefarious activities, and the U.S. should update their designations to disrupt their efforts. Lack of sanctions enforcement could be interpreted to mean that U.S. countermeasures may be short lived. U.S. credibility and deterrence are at stake.

CONCLUSION AND RECOMMENDATIONS

Mr. Chairman, sanctions and designations alone cannot be expected to put an end to Hezbollah's financial operations in the Western Hemisphere. However, they help, especially when combined with other tools.

1. Hit Hezbollah with the full arsenal of U.S. sanctions and law enforcement tools.

Congress should swiftly reconcile the House and Senate version of HIFPAA 2017 and send the bill to the president. HIFPAA is an excellent tool because it combines and complements in one bill all existing tools, including sanctions, designations, and prosecutions. By passing HIFPAA 2017, Congress will make the Kingpin Act and other existing tools more effective.

2. Sanction Hezbollah and its senior leadership with TCO and Kingpin designations.

Hezbollah is a terror organization. But it also runs a global criminal enterprise that trades illicit drugs. On this ground, I strongly recommend that the U.S. administration designate Hezbollah as both a Transnational Criminal Organization and a Global Kingpin. Both designations should not stop at the organizational level but should be extended to Hezbollah's senior leadership involved in deciding, endorsing, religiously justifying, coordinating, and benefiting from the traffic of illicit substances.

3. Couple Hezbollah terror finance designations with TCO and Kingpin designations.

My next recommendation is to couple terror finance designations, such as the ones used in 2004 and 2006 against Hezbollah TBA operatives, with Kingpin designations. It is important to emphasize the fact that designated terror-finance operatives for Hezbollah are involved in criminal activities on behalf of a global criminal franchise. They should carry this multiple stigma.

Such designations have other practical implications, especially in countries where Hezbollah is not considered a terrorist organization, which is the case with all countries in Latin America. Local governments will be reluctant to prosecute terror financiers but may respond more positively to U.S. requests to arrest, prosecute, and extradite individuals implicated in drug trafficking and

---

formed to violate any of the prohibitions set forth in this part is prohibited." Hizballah Financial Sanctions Regulations, 31 e-C.F.R. §566.601, November 2, 2017. (https://www.ecfr.gov/cgi-bin/text-idx?SID=235c0575169e66186fc81e00eeaf83fc&mc=true&node=pt31.3.566&rgn=div5#se31.3.566_1202).

Emanuele Ottolenghi   November 8, 2017

organized crime. Even if designations alone cannot achieve much, they can create the groundwork for successful law enforcement prosecutions.

4. Target enablers with Global Magnitsky and HIFPAA.

Mr. Chairman, a large factor explaining Hezbollah's success is its reliance on influence and access to local politicians, law enforcement, judges and prosecutors, airport security, and other officials in Latin American countries to buy their silence and complicity. If proven true, the U.S. government can rely on the Global Magnitsky Act of 2016 to punish a foreign dignitary's corrupt practices. The legislation specifically empowers the chairperson and ranking member of a committee from either house of Congress to request that the president investigates, within 120 days, cases of corruption by government officials. Such a request, with regards to for example certain officials in the Tri-Border Area and other jurisdictions where Hezbollah is active, would be entirely appropriate and within the authorities granted to Congress by the Global Magnitsky Act.

The new Hezbollah bill, currently being reconciled, would also enable the administration to punish this official, and others engaged in similarly corrupt practices, with additional measures. Indeed, corruption and complicity through the provision of services can now be punished with a variety of measures, including the denial or revocation of visas to the United States.

HIFPAA also would reduce the threshold for designations to extend to those who, while not conclusively proven to be members of Hezbollah, are clearly facilitators and enablers of its activities. This measure would permit U.S. authorities to go after companies, financial institutions, accounting and legal firms, virtual office service providers, and others who enable Hezbollah's terror finance. For these actors, it will be more difficult to continue to operate outside the financial system once the U.S. slaps sanctions on them.

5. Impose a 311 designation on financial institutions known to be assisting Hezbollah in Latin America.

Mr. Chairman, the continuing business activities of individuals and entities sanctioned by the United States occur because local governments are either reluctant to implement U.S. sanctions or actively cooperate with the terrorists. The administration should demand that they either comply or face consequences. These should include imposing 311 designations[105] on financial institutions known to be used by Hezbollah financiers to move their revenues, designating banking sectors of countries that facilitate Hezbollah's terror finance as zones of primary money laundering concern, and working within international forums like the Financial Action Task Force to have such countries blacklisted.

6. Empower law enforcement to go after Hezbollah's global financial networks.

Mr. Chairman, sanctions have had some salutary effect. They have named and shamed individuals, companies, and organizations. They have cut off terror entities from the U.S. financial system.

---

[105] U.S. Department of the Treasury, Press Release, "Fact Sheet: Overview of Section 311 of the USA PATRIOT Act." February 10. 2011. (https://www.treasury.gov/press-center/press-releases/Pages/tg1056.aspx)

Emanuele Ottolenghi   November 8, 2017

They have nudged U.S. allies and the global financial system into compliance. Nevertheless, there are enough countries that disagree with or disregard U.S. policy. Hezbollah terrorists find a haven where U.S. sanctions alone have limited reach.

Law enforcement has demonstrated how it can complement sanctions. The cases I mentioned in my written statement all involve a balance of sanctions and prosecution. The combination of tools always works as a force multiplier with coordination among agencies, and a shared goal of disrupting Hezbollah's cash flows drive policy.

Step one, then, must surely be to appoint a new DEA administrator. In the midst of an opioid crisis and with cocaine from Latin America flooding the U.S., it should be a high priority for the administration to appoint a strong candidate who has the vision and the experience to go after transnational criminal organizations such as Hezbollah and has the skills to coordinate government agencies, navigate bureaucracy, and build friendships and alliances internationally to be able to rely on foreign agencies' cooperation in running international investigations.

As understanding the full scope of this complicated global network is difficult for even the most seasoned investigators, step two should be to empower the new DEA administrator with the necessary tools and resources to create specialized units with skillsets to aggressively apply all tools available to law enforcement. Simultaneously, those teams could work with sanctioning entities and allied foreign governments for a comprehensive U.S.-led approach in dismantling regional sub-networks for overall impact.

7. Give more resources to Treasury.

Finally, Mr. Chairman, Treasury needs more resources. OFAC cannot work cases through the system without access to more resources that can enable the bureaucracy to work faster and cast its net wider.

Hezbollah, Mr. Chairman, is a global threat. As John Feltman and Daniel Benjamin said in a joint testimony to the Senate Foreign Relations Committee's subcommittee on Near Eastern and South and Central Asian Affairs in June 2010:

> Hezbollah has ... broadened its sources of financial support in recent years. Hezbollah is now heavily involved in a wide range of criminal activity, including the drug trade and smuggling. It also receives funds from both legitimate and illicit businesses that its members operate, from NGOs under its control, and from donations from its supporters throughout the world.[106]

The U.S., too, needs to broaden its tools to confront this multifaceted enemy. All tools of tradecraft are needed to confront this threat.

Thank you for the opportunity to testify. I look forward to the committee's questions.

---

[106] "Assessing the Strength of Hezbollah." *Hearing before the Subcommittee on Near Eastern and South and Central Asian Affairs of the Senate Committee on Foreign Relations,* June 8, 2010. (https://www.gpo.gov/fdsys/pkg/CHRG-111shrg62141/pdf/CHRG-111shrg62141.pdf)

Mr. COOK. Thank you, very much, Doctor.

Finally, let me introduce Mr. Eric Olson. Mr. Olson is deputy director of the Latin American Program and senior adviser to the Mexican Institute at the Woodrow Wilson International Center for Scholars in Washington, DC. Thank you for joining us today. You are recognized for 5 minutes.

STATEMENT OF MR. ERIC L. OLSON, DEPUTY DIRECTOR, LATIN AMERICAN PROGRAM, WOODROW WILSON CENTER

Mr. OLSON. Thank you, Chairman Cook, and congratulations on your appointment. And thank you to Ranking Member Sires and the other members of the committee for this opportunity to appear before you today on behalf of the Wilson Center.

Given the limited time I have, I would like to focus my remarks on the policy ideas and suggestions I set forward in my written testimony which I have submitted for the record.

To begin, I want to make clear that I believe the Foreign Narcotics Kingpin Designation Act of 1991 is one of the most important and powerful instruments the United States has in its quiver to fight organized crime and illicit financing in the region. It has been used to good effect against powerful criminal organizations and persons in countries such as Colombia Venezuela, Mexico, and throughout Central America. Since implementation began in 2000, there have been approximately 1800 persons and entities designated and sanctioned under the act. The vast majority, as you pointed out, are in the Western Hemisphere.

While the use has been far-reaching, a full review of the effectiveness of this program and policy has not been conducted yet. As far as I know, neither the Treasury Department's Office of Inspector General, nor the Government Accountability Office, has conducted a full analysis nor has there been a full policy review within Treasury. As far as I know, this hearing is the first attempt to look broadly at this policy and whether it is effective or not.

The time is right to request a full, objective, and data-driven evaluation of the act's effectiveness. It has been nearly 17 years since it has been first implemented. So it is time to do a cost-benefit analysis and to find out if the act is as effective as anecdotes might suggest it is. And we all have good and positive anecdotes about its effectiveness, but it is time for a broad analysis and evaluation.

Questions that must be answered include whether the Kingpin Act is effectively dismantling criminal organizations or simply splitting them up and fragmenting them. Is it having any measurable impact on accountability for criminal networks and their bosses in the region? We can point to prosecutions and convictions in the United States. But, as the Honduras example that has been referred to here, and I talk about it in my written testimony, suggest, involving the Rosenthal family and Continental Bank, there really has not been much accountability for them in Honduras.

Secondly, we need to use this powerful tool in a focused and careful way, seeking to avoid damage to legitimate elements of financial systems and economies in our drive to root out criminals. This is particularly the case, again, in small, weak countries such as

Honduras where sudden designations can put at risk entire financial systems and economies.

The designation of the Rosenthal family in Honduras and the Continental Bank is a case in point. There is overwhelming evidence that the bank and Rosenthal family were involved in money laundering on behalf of the Cachiros criminal group. But since this was the first time a bank itself was designated under the act, it caused near panic within the country's financial system, with many people refusing to conduct even permitted transactions with other banks for fear of somehow crossing the line and putting themselves and their business in jeopardy. And I think this refers a little bit to what Mr. Hall was talking about, this strict liability provision, good faith not being good enough. People panic and worry not about Banco Continental, which deserved to be dismantled, but broader financial issues and questions in that country.

Third, we need to use the leverage provided by the Kingpin Act to ensure that countries undertake broader reforms of their financial and judicial systems. Sanctioning individuals and entities are powerful tools. But if we can use the leverage that comes with the sanctions to push for broader reforms, greater transparency, and accountability, the benefits can be immense.

Fourth, we should continue investing in efforts to strengthen the capacity of financial oversight and regulatory institutions in the region. It was an open secret in Honduras that the Rosenthal family and Continental Bank were allegedly involved in money laundering activities. Everybody talked about it. It was even published in the newspaper. But nothing happened. And the Honduran National Commission for Banks and Insurance claimed to be completely surprised by this designation. So we need to do more to improve their capacity to do oversight and not just depend on our action.

I know I am out of time, but I have two really quick more recommendations. One, top down, high-value target strategies can be valuable when confronting organized crime but they often lead to fragmentation of criminal networks that metastasize, often forming new criminal groups or joining others in the process. And we need to view this as one amongst many instruments to attack organized crime.

And, finally, as this tool has become the centerpiece of the administration's strategy for countering transnational organized crime, Congress needs to make sure there are adequate resources and trained personnel to conduct the investigations and enforce the sanctions that form the backbone of these designations under the act.

Thank you very much.

[The prepared statement of Mr. Olson follows:]

Statement By

Eric L. Olson

Deputy Director, Latin American Program

Senior Advisor, Mexico Institute

Woodrow Wilson International Center for Scholars

Subcommittee on Western Hemisphere
House Committee on Foreign Affairs
United States House of Representatives

November 8, 2017

**"Examining the Effectiveness of the Kingpin Designation Act
in the Western Hemisphere"**

Good afternoon, Chairman Cook, Ranking Member Sires, and Members of the Committee. Thank you for the opportunity to appear before you today on behalf of the Woodrow Wilson Center.

As you may know, the Wilson Center was created by an act of Congress as our nation's living memorial to President Woodrow Wilson. In the words of Vice President Pence, the Wilson Center is "an institution of independent research and open dialogue and actionable ideas, truly a bi-partisan stalwart here in Washington D.C."

With that in mind, I offer the following thoughts and suggestions regarding the effectiveness of the Foreign Narcotics Kingpin Designation Act:

To begin, I believe Kingpin Designation Act of 1999 is one of the most important and powerful instruments the United States has in its quiver to fight organized crime networks and illicit financing in the region. Since the Treasury Department's Office of Foreign Assets Control issued the Foreign Narcotics Kingpin Sanctions Regulations in 2000 there have been approximately 1800 persons and entities designated and sanctioned under the act. The vast majority of these are from the Western Hemisphere.

The act is intended to paralyze a criminal group by going after its illicit properties and proceeds with the goal to take the "benefit" out of their illicit activities. One of the intended byproducts of a Kingpin designation is to produce a pariah effect to dissuade legitimate businesses from becoming enmeshed in illicit activity, or seen another way, to make it more difficult for criminal organizations to launder their illicit proceeds through legitimate businesses.

While its use has been far reaching, and many of the region's most important drug traffickers and money launders have been sanctioned under its authority, there has not been, to my knowledge, a full review of the effectiveness of the program and policy. In 2007, the Office of Foreign Assets Control conducted its own internal review of the Colombia-specific narcotics-sanctions program, but this was not a comprehensive review of the Act or an independent review. When the Kingpin Act was enacted it also created a Foreign Assets Judicial Review Commission that looks into legal questions related to the Act's implementation. But I'm unaware of any public report from the Commission. Furthermore, there has been no analysis from the Treasury Department's Office of Inspector General, and nothing from the Government Accountability Office.

So an initial recommendation might be to encourage a full policy review and objective evaluation of what has been a widely used and presumably successful element of United States policy and strategy to counter transnational organized crime.

Speaking anecdotally, there is no question that the Act has been used to good effect in several countries such as Venezuela, Colombia, and Mexico. It has also been used in Central America on several occasions and in particular Honduras where I would like to focus my comments. While I have not conducted a full review of the effectiveness of the Act's use in the Western Hemisphere, I believe there are some important insights to glean from the Honduras case.

Background on the *Banco Continental* and Rosenthal family case

On October 7, 2015, the Treasury Department's Office of Foreign Assets Control designated three members of the Rosenthal family of Honduras, the country's sixth largest Bank (Banco Continental), and several related businesses under the Kingpin Act. According to the Office of Foreign Assets Control it was the first time a bank had been designated under the Act.

Jaime Rosenthal Oliva, one of Honduras's richest and most powerful men, headed the Rosenthal family businesses. Not only did he and his family control Banco Continental, but he is the former Vice President Honduras, and owner of one of the country's most important national newspapers – *El Tiempo*.

As part of the same designation, Mr. Rosenthal's son, **Yani Rosenthal**, and nephew, **Yankel Rosenthal Coello,** were also named. All three were sanctioned for "playing a significant role in international narcotics trafficking … including providing money laundering and other services…" to several Central American drug trafficking and criminal organizations, most notably the so-called "Cachiros." The Cachiros had previously been designated under the Act in September 2013.

Again, it's worth noting that these are not just alleged criminal actors but powerful political characters in their own right. Yani Rosenthal served as a member of the Honduran Congress from 2010 to 2014, and before that was Minister of the Presidency from 2006 to 2007. He was a candidate for President of Honduras in both the 2009 and 2013 elections. Yankel Rosenthal Coello, was Honduras's Minister of Investment until June 2015 and was president of Marathon, one of Honduras's strongest soccer clubs.

Yani Rosenthal plead guilty to money laundering in New York's Southern District Court on July 26, 2017, and Yankel Rosenthal Coello plead guilty to attempted money laundering in New York Southern District Court on August 29, 2017. Sentencing is scheduled for January 2018.

According to their indictment by the U.S. Department of Justice, The Rosenthals allegedly used a variety of mechanisms to launder Cachiros' money, including using Banco Continental to issue loans to the Cachiros, which were paid back with drug money. Banco Continental also allegedly helped Cachiros leaders establish other businesses, including the Joya Grande Zoo, and to buy equipment for construction, mining, and African palm oil companies. Some of the money laundered by the

Cachiros through the Bank allegedly came from the Government of Honduras in payment for infrastructure projects.

Jaime Rosenthal remains in Honduras, where he is on trial for unrelated charges of fraud that stem back to 2004. The United States issued a request for his extradition at the end of December 2015, but the Supreme Court of Honduras ruled that Rosenthal's charges in Honduras must be resolved before he can be extradited to the United States. Although the case against him in Honduras dates back to 2004, Rosenthal's trial has been postponed multiple times, and is currently scheduled to resume on November 30, 2017. I would point out that Honduras holds national elections on November 26th.

Benefits of the Rosenthal Money Laundering Organization Designation.

So what are the benefits of this designation for the fight against criminal organizations, corruption, and impunity in Honduras?

- While final court determinations have yet to be made, it's clear that this designation struck a powerful blow not only against the Rosenthal family's alleged criminal enterprises, but also against the Cachiros and other criminal networks in Honduras and throughout Central America. One of the linchpins of their criminal enterprise was crippled and destroyed.
- A number of very powerful but corrupt economic and political actors in Honduras where taken off the playing field, and their ability to manipulate and distort Honduran governance, the economy, and society was seriously weakened.
- This was a wakeup call to Honduran agencies charged with fighting money laundering and organized crime – especially the Honduran National Bank and Insurance Commission.

What can be gleaned from this experience?

One of the troubling aspects of the Banco Continental case is that the alleged links between the Bank, the Rosenthal family, Honduran politicians, and criminal organizations such as the Cachiros had long been an open secret. Not only did I hear often about these links but investigative journalists where writing and publishing reports and stories about this apparent link. For example, see "Insight Crime's" report: **Honduras Elites and Organized Crime: The Cachiros.** April 9, 2016.

Despite this and other evidence, Honduras's bank oversight board and Attorney's General Office did not take action until the designation was made by the Office of Foreign Assets Control.

In contrast to Mexico and Colombia, Honduras is a small and fragile country with weak governance capacity and a tiny economy. There are many ways in which the line between organized crime and the state have become blurred. Economic and political elite can become vehicles for corruption that have lasting impact on the country's governance.

So designations such as these in Honduras have the potential to create broader uncertainty, even a sense of panic that could potentially undermine a country's entire economy. As mentioned, the designation included a bank that (corrupt or not) was enmeshed in a broader financial system, so sanctioning and dissolving the Banco Continental, as happened in this case, had the potential to bring down a lot of people and financial institutions whether they were part of a criminal conspiracy or not. This is less likely to be the case when individuals and businesses are sanctioned and in larger countries like Colombia and Mexico.

While there is good reason for Treasury to employ the element of surprise, in part because our counterparts are not always reliable, as suggested above, there are also risks. In this specific case the sudden announcement of sanctions by the Treasury Department against an important national bank created a sense of uncertainty within the Honduran financial system and legitimate depositors over whether further actions by Treasury could be expected.

Furthermore, even though the Kingpin Act's reach is largely limited to U.S. persons, many foreign citizens can refuse to engage in transactions that have been prohibited for U.S. persons.[1] According to this analysis, "even if a foreign entity can engage in certain business, if that business is sensitive for U.S. persons because of OFAC regulations, then oftentimes the foreign entity will want nothing to do with the transaction."[2] For this reason, the Treasury Department had to issue a clarification on their action on October 11th so that legitimate transactions by non-U.S. persons would not become paralyzed in the process, and thus put at risk the broader financial system.[3]

Bottom line, while the tool is powerful and legitimate, it carries with it the risk of collateral damage that can potentially undermine legitimate sectors of the financial system and ultimately the economy.

---

[1] See "OFAC Clarifies its Position on a Foreign Bank: What this Says about 3rd Country Actors," blog post by Farhad Alavi, October 11, 2015, in Ussanctions.com. Access here: https://ussanctions.com/2015/10/11/ofac-clarifies-its-position-on-a-foreign-bank-the-case-of-banco-continental/

[2] Ibid.

[3] Department of the Treasury, Office of Foreign Assets Control: Statement of Proposed Liquidation of Banco Continental. See here: https://www.treasury.gov/resource-center/sanctions/Programs/Documents/banco_continental_10112015.pdf

Policy Options for the Future:

Based on this case and consultations with many experts I would offer the following options for consideration by the Subcommittee and Congress.

1) The time is right to request a full, objective, data driven evaluation of the effectiveness of the Kingpin Act. It's now been nearly seventeen years since it was first implemented and it is time to do a cost benefit analysis, and to find out if the Act is as effective as anecdotes might suggest it is. Questions that must be answered include whether the Kingpin Act is having any measurable impact on accountability for criminal networks and their bosses in the region? We can point to prosecutions and convictions in the United States but as the Rosenthal case suggestion, we may not be seeing greater accountability in the region.

2) We need to use this powerful tool in a focused and careful way, seeking to avoid damaging the legitimate elements of financial systems and economies in our drive to root out criminals.

3) We need to use the leverage provided by the Kingpin Act to ensure that countries undertake broader reforms of their financial and judicial systems. Sanctioning individuals and entities are powerful tools but if we can use the leverage that comes with the sanctions to push for broader reforms, the benefits can be immense.

4) We need to continue investing in efforts to strengthen the capacity of financial oversight institutions in the region. The apparent lack of action and urgency in the Honduran National Commission for Banks and Insurance is deeply troubling. Some inaction is due to lack of capacity, but in can also be the result of lack of political will to address the obvious problems of penetration of the state by powerful criminal, economic, and political leaders.

5) Top down high value target strategies can be valuable when confronting organized crime but they often lead to the fragmentation of criminal networks that metastasize, often forming new criminal groups or joining others. These can lead to increased competition between rival criminal groups increasing violence, insecurity, and instability. In our zeal to capture the big fish, we should not overlook the benefits of building security from the bottom-up, closing off space for criminal groups to work at the local level, cutting off their access to political, economic, and social control in villages, towns, and small cities that form the foundation of their enterprise.

6) Finally, as this tool has become the centerpiece of the Administration's strategy for countering transnational organized crime, Congress needs to make sure there are adequate resources and trained personnel to conduct the investigations and enforce the sanctions that form the backbone of the designations under the Kingpin Act.
Thank you and I am happy to take your questions.

———————

Mr. COOK. Thank you, very much, sir.

I want to thank the panel for being very good on time. It goes fast, doesn't it? And I don't have this clock up here where I speed it up. I don't cheat, really. So, anyway, I do want to compliment you, and I didn't want to start off my first meeting being the bad guy.

Anyway, I yield myself 5 minutes to ask some questions. And, full disclosure, you know, today we had a birthday ceremony for the Marine Corps birthday. It is 242 years old. And I am old, but I am not that old. But, anyway, when I was listening to the testimony, I always remember the terrorist incident in Lebanon where my own battalion, First Battalion Eighth Marines, had over 200 Marines, soldiers and sailors, that were killed, many more wounded, and the question of international terrorism.

And a couple of the gentlemen referred to Hezbollah and its activities. I think when you talk to the average American on the street, they don't think of that organization being in the Western Hemisphere. They think of it as being in the Middle East, maybe North Africa or what have you. And this opens up a whole new area.

And if you mention that, but I wanted to see if anyone was going to mention on how we can do more and suggestions on how we can implement that in terms of that organization obviously being international and to be under the Kingpin Act. Anyone? Yes, sir?

Mr. OTTOLENGHI. If I may. Thank you for your question.

I mean, the amount of actions that could be taken is very significant. Their presence all over the Western Hemisphere is very important and growing. Hezbollah's assessed estimated annual operating budget is in the ballpark of at least $1 billion and at least 30 percent of that comes from global illicit activities, chiefly drug trading. It is one of the principal sources of cocaine both in Europe and increasingly in the United States as a middleman for the cartels. That is why it is so important and directly impacting, I think, to U.S. national interests.

And just one point of the many things that I would note is that Hezbollah is active in Latin America. I mentioned the tri-border area of Argentina, Brazil, Paraguay. There is also significant activity in Venezuela, in the Caribbean islands, in Panama, and elsewhere. In many of these places, Hezbollah operatives manage to acquire, through corruption or because of lax immigration schemes, dual nationalities from those countries which allow them to operate a lot more freely in the financial systems and in the jurisdictions in which they find themselves. So working with regional allies to look into the way that these criminals are easily acquiring citizenship in those countries would be one step forward.

Thank you.

Mr. COOK. Thank you.

Anyone else want to comment on that? Sir?

Mr. SEMESKY. Yes. Mr. Chairman, I would add, first of all, I would agree with everything that Dr. Ottolenghi just stated and also point out that when Hezbollah started to become a global organization, it already had somewhat of an infrastructure in place in the Lebanese diaspora around the world, and especially in the free trade zones in Latin America. If you look at the Panama free trade zone, the trade zones in Chile and Peru, all throughout Latin America, and the tri-border, as the doctor mentioned, many businessmen and many that have been connected as financiers or contributors, sympathizers.

So the fact of free trade zones are especially alarming in that trade goods, illicit goods, weapons of mass destruction, can move through those trade zones almost unnoticed in those countries with very weak infrastructure. So I think to the extent that the U.S. can stay on top of the trade movement throughout Latin America, that would be a recommendation.

Mr. COOK. I just want to make a comment before I recognize the ranking member. You know, 2 years ago, 1 year ago, we were talking about ISIS, Daesh, or ISIL, whatever you want to call them, but the fact that the corruption and the illegal smuggling of, or selling oil on the black market, all those things, I think that variable was highlighted in different organizations, task force went after that, and I am just thinking hopefully we can capitalize on some of those lessons learned and use in this war against some of these organizations.

So my time has expired. And, Mr. Sires, you are recognized.

Mr. SIRES. Thank you, Mr. Chairman.

When we designate a senior member of a criminal organization, does that shed any light on the connection between the organization and the corrupt government officials that they work with? Mr. Semesky? Looks like nobody else wants to——

Mr. SEMESKY. It sheds light, sir, in that it helps as the information and the data is gathered, embedded through the interagency, and different agencies start taking other agencies' information and running it through their systems, the knowledge of the organization actually expands. And a lot of times those designations cause investigations or are the result of investigations, which then could bring to light government corruption connected to those drug cartels or money laundering organizations.

Mr. OTTOLENGHI. If I may add one point which applies to Hezbollah, but I guess in general to other criminal organizations. Generally speaking, a lot of these transnational organized crime activities, chiefly the moving of illicit substances, require the complicity and the collusions of a significant number of public officials at all levels, whether it is customs, or, you know, airport security officials, border police, prosecutors, judges. And organized crime across the world has the habit of buying access and influence at the highest levels of power in order to facilitate these activities.

Now, corruption is rampant in Latin America. So I think that the use of these instruments does not only facilitate the exposure of the connection between crime and power, but it also opens up the possibility that the United States can use instruments such as the Kingpin Act, such as the Global Magnitsky, to go after corrupt officials who are the enablers of crime when we cannot go after the criminals themselves.

Mr. SIRES. Thank you.

I am dying to ask this question. Because we had a meeting with the President of Colombia, and they were working on a deal with the FARC, and I asked him have they found any money hidden of the FARC. And he told us no, there is no money. Does anybody——

all four of you, do you believe that or am I just being a little skep-
tical I guess?

Mr. SEMESKY. Congressman Sires, your skepticism is well placed.
There is money. And we are continually working with the Colombian Government and the interagency to identify it. Because the
FARC is a guerrilla organization, because they do operate in the
jungles, and do operate with cash, it is very difficult until it hits
the financial system. And then you have to find it. Their biggest
expense, obviously, is their infrastructure and payment for their
soldiers. And they do spend a lot of their revenue through that re-
quirement.

But we do believe there are hundreds of millions, or billions, of
dollars in their hands which we are constantly trying to identify.

Mr. SIRES. Well, the reason I ask that question is because now
these people are allowed to participate in the process of the election
in the future. And, quite frankly, if you have that money hidden,
you can actually buy the election in the future with all of the
money. So we win the battle and lose the war. So I was quite dis-
appointed, you know, with that response.

And the question is, if you get on the list, how do you get off it?

Mr. OLSON. I will defer to them, because I think they know exactly much more how to do that.

Mr. SEMESKY. Congressman, there is a process in place to be removed from the list. And OFAC had taken quite a few people off
the list over the years. Typically, a tier one designee is the actual
kingpin. Under that kingpin are associated entities which could be
individuals or businesses. And, typically, it is almost impossible for
a tier 1 entity to be removed from the list. However, if an individual or a business can prove to OFAC, that they have severed
ties, they are no longer associating, and have divested themselves
of their assets in joint financial endeavors, OFAC will remove them
from the list. And they do advertise that.

Mr. SIRES. Thank you, Mr. Chairman. My time is up.

Mr. COOK. Thank you, very much.

I am now going to recognize Congressman Donovan from New
York.

Mr. DONOVAN. Thank you, Mr. Chairman.

And thank you for your enlightened testimony. I was a drug
prosecutor in New York City for 8 years, and then I was the elected
district attorney, chief prosecutor, one of the five in New York City,
before I came to Congress. Much of our success was the seizing of
assets of the people who we were pursuing. I guess it was part of
their trade when they knew they were going to lose product. But
it was when we took their assets that we really harmed them.

How successful do you think we are being in identifying assets
and in cases seizing them with the people who are on the list that
you have provided for us?

Mr. SEMESKY. As far as the people on the list, I would say overall
not very successful. I will say that when a country follows the list—
in Colombia it is known as the Clinton list because President
Clinton signed the initial legislation. And it is also known as civil
death. If you are on the list, you do not have access to the financial
system. And as I pointed out, the Rodriguez Orejuelas turned

themselves in specifically to get their families removed from the list.

At DEA, what we have done is when we investigate financial cases, we have a money flow strategy where we use money more as a weapon against the cartels than as a tool for asset forfeiture, although we do take as much money as we can identify, and that is the money flows back toward sources of supply. The drugs flow toward the abusers. Our investigations prioritize the flow of money back to the sources of supply so we can identify command and control of those organizations.

And it also helps us infiltrate the organizations. The panel members mentioned the case with Ayman Joumaa. That started with a DEA money laundering investigation where we provided services. We infiltrated the organization, and we ended up taking down quite a few drug traffickers, money launderers, and a bank in Lebanon.

Mr. OLSON. I would just add to that—I don't know if I am on here. I would just add to that that one of the reasons I think it is important—and I include it in my recommendations—that we work with our partners in the region to strengthen their own capacity is that a lot of times we are dealing with Attorney Generals offices that are weak. We are dealing with other bank oversight commissions that are weak in the region. And it limits what we can do from a law enforcement point of view and from an effectiveness point of view.

The Kingpin Act is strong, and it is good. There are ways to make it better. But it is one tool amongst many. And if our partner in our other countries aren't strong, and capable, and honest, and transparent, it really weakens and undermines our own ability to go after the assets of, say, the FARC or other criminal organizations. Now, I would say Colombia has a pretty strong and improved financial system compared to other countries in the region. But, nevertheless, I think this is one of the things we can't lose sight of. We have a strong tool but sometimes the countries don't themselves.

Some of the countries in Central America are just now adopting asset forfeiture laws and just beginning the process of implementing those laws. It is new to them. And so I think we can't lose sight of that important aspect of this whole equation.

Mr. DONOVAN. You hit on my second question. I only have a minute, so I offer it to the rest of the members of the panel. How can we improve the kingpin statute? What can we do to achieve our goals of the statute in a better way after it has been implemented and enacted nearly 20 years now?

Mr. SEMESKY. Congressman, to me, it is a very effective statute and sanctions program. The most significant way you can improve it is to add more resources to the office that administers it. They are woefully understaffed. They do not have the people to do the investigations, to work with the agencies. They do to the extent they can, and I think the resources—if you looked—and I can't tell you what they are. But I know that they are very, very much understaffed right now. So I think that would go a long way. When they have the people to do the work, it is a very effective program.

Mr. DONOVAN. I thank you all. Mr. Chairman, my time has expired. Thank you.

Mr. COOK. Thank you very much.

Now I am going to recognize the gentlelady from Illinois.

Ms. KELLY. Thank you, Mr. Chair. And I thank my colleague for letting me go ahead of her.

Mr. Olson, you said something very interesting. You talked about we need to evaluate what we have been doing, and you talked about it really doing what it has said it is doing or is it just serving to dismantle and fragment the bad guys, I guess. And it made me think about—I represent the Chicagoland area, and that is the same thing that has been said about the gangs, that they put the head of the gangs in jail and now the gangs are fragmented and they are fighting for 2-block territories. And you see the chaos that has been in Chicago.

But, Mr. Hall, you said that the 50 percent rule almost guarantees that the U.S. Government will fail in achieving its own goal. What would you change in order to balance the rule with the government's goal?

Mr. HALL. I would eliminate the rule in its entirety. I think what needs to happen—this blends into what we have just been talking about in terms of effectiveness. Because if you think about how, in reality, on the ground, sanctions rules get enforced in the United States, it is at the business level. It is at the individual business level. And the companies that are trying to comply don't have the resources that the Federal Government has. And, actually, they rarely understand why a particular entity is even sanctioned. All they know is that it is and they are not supposed to deal with them. They are trying to figure out whether the person they are dealing with, who might have a similar name or similar business name is the same entity.

So all that ambiguity leads to ineffectiveness in enforcement. And it leads companies to a position where they are just guessing. So, you know, the more granularity the government offers business in terms of identifying sanctioned individuals and entities, the more effective the program is going to be. By just sort of issuing a blanket edict that says, you know, any entity that is 50 percent owned by other—in the aggregate—other sanctioned entities that aren't named, that is guaranteed to lead to failure. So that is what I meant by that.

Ms. KELLY. Do you know how many businesses in the United States have been affected by the Rule?

Mr. HALL. I am only aware of one enforcement action under the rule. And that was about 1 year ago. That was in 2016. Now, I don't know why there has only been one. I guess it is not that old of a rule, for one thing. But, for another, you know, it makes me wonder if the government knows—if the government has spent enough time and resources figuring out the ownership structures of these 50 percent owned entities and whether they know which entities are 50 percent or more owned by an aggregation of other sanctioned entities. It is a hard problem to solve. But it is a problem that intelligence agencies and law enforcement agencies have the resources to address.

Ms. KELLY. And is there anything you would put in its place or just forget about it?

Mr. HALL. No. I would not replace it. I think the 50 percent rule is—it is just fundamentally the wrong approach to tell individual businesses, you have to figure this out. We are the Government, you know, we haven't figured it out, we are going to put it on you, and then, if you make a mistake, we are going to enforce the sanctions against you on a strict liability basis with penalties, you know, on the—you know, of over $¼ million per transaction, which adds up.

Ms. KELLY. Okay. Well, I think the idea of a full and objective data-driven evaluation would be an excellent idea since you said nothing has been done in 17 years. And maybe that will get to your point.

Mr. HALL. No, I think that is a really good recommendation. I was actually shocked to hear that.

Ms. KELLY. Did you have—oh, I didn't know if you were——

Mr. SEMESKY. I am sorry, Congresswoman. I was just going to add that I don't completely agree with Mr. Hall on that point. And if I—the 50 percent rule is—I understand where he is coming from, and it is not fair to business. But also if OFAC discovers a business that is owned 50 percent and it isn't on the list, if they didn't have that rule, they wouldn't be able to freeze its assets.

Ms. KELLY. Okay.

Mr. SEMESKY. Now, I do agree with the strict liability, the problem that creates for businesses. And it isn't fair. Okay? There should be some type of mitigation guidelines in place that if you truly do not know, you cooperate once you discover it, you self-disclose, there shouldn't be penalties.

So, I mean, I would add that I don't agree with the one but I do agree with the other.

Ms. KELLY. Thank you. My time is out.

Thank you.

Mr. COOK. Thank you very much.

I am now going to recognize the gentleman from Florida, Mr. Rooney.

Mr. ROONEY. Thank you, Mr. Chairman.

Mr. COOK. Thank you, sir.

Mr. ROONEY. I might comment right quick about that, being a business guy. You know, there are self-disclosure procedures in the EPA and the DOJ for companies when they discover something like a blowout preventer failure on an oil well, or something, to immediately call them and say we have got this problem and that gets them out of the strict liability kind of thing. So it might be something to think about.

I would like to ask Dr. Ottolenghi. If the EON and the AUC are both designated foreign terrorist organizations, how come we are not designating the ELN as well?

Mr. OTTOLENGHI. First of all, thank you for your question. I wouldn't be opposed, of course. I think that is a question for the administration, though, to be asked whether that organization should also fall under the sanctions program.

If I may add a point about what you just said regarding ownership, which goes back to the activities of these organizations. By design, a lot of these companies will be opaque. There will be an intentional deliberate obfuscation of what these organizations are about. And that usually starts with ownership. And so effective control, which requires a lot of investigation on the parts of the Government to determine who really is behind these entities, I think would be the defining factor for listing and/or delisting entities.

Mr. ROONEY. So is there anything to do with the FARC agreement and the Government of Colombia's desires to make sure that thing proceeds forward and are not designating ELN, maybe for anybody that has an opinion.

Mr. OLSON. I mean, I think the designation is up to the Treasury Department, so it doesn't—it is not a matter of whether the Colombian Government wants it or not.

Mr. ROONEY. Other than subtle——

Mr. OLSON. Well, yeah. I mean, I think there is obviously a desire to, on the part of the Colombian Government to bring this, you know, process to an end as quickly as possible. But I think it is up to the Treasury Department whether they would designate the ELN. And my understanding is, in the past, the assumption was that ELN, while a communist guerrilla group and all that sort of stuff, they were a little bit different than the FARC. And I am not taking sides here, but—in that they were less involved with drug trafficking. And that was what the Kingpin Act was designed to deal with.

Now, that could very well have changed. There may be reason to reevaluate that. All those sorts of things could be true. But that would really be, you know, a Treasury and ultimately State Department involvement in that assessment, and DEA I am sure.

Mr. ROONEY. Yeah. I don't know.

The other question I would like to ask Dr. Ottolenghi is about— you have a lot in your report—very great report, by the way. Thank you.

Mr. OTTOLENGHI. Thank you.

Mr. ROONEY. I am going to say that—about the role of Hezbollah all throughout Latin America. And I just would figure that Iran is there everywhere Hezbollah is. I wonder if you would like to elaborate a little bit from your experience about the role of Iran backed Hezbollah in Latin America and some of the things Iran is doing independently of Hezbollah, like in Venezuela and Nicaragua.

Mr. OTTOLENGHI. I have to entirely second what you just said. Wherever Hezbollah goes, there is Iran, and usually vice versa. And my understanding is that, in many of the illicit traffic networks that Hezbollah is running in Latin America, there is usually either a liaison person or some sort of a political commissar from Iran, and it doesn't necessarily have to be an Iranian person. It could be a Lebanese member of Hezbollah that acts as an integrated member of the Quds force running that. So oftentimes we have to see these activities as integral to what Iran is doing in Latin America.

Now, in addition to that, as you pointed out, Iran does things also independently of these traffics. And I think that, you know, Iran, in the case of Venezuela, as you mentioned, is very important, but in other countries as well. Iran has been trying, for 3, almost

4 decades, to gain influence across the entire region. It does so by establishing alliances with like-minded political movements, and it is very pragmatic in the way it chooses interlocutors. They can be on pretty much the whole political spectrum.

It provides them with financing, with assistance, with training in order eventually to gain access to political power if they eventually become parts of the government.

It is spreading its influence through soft power tools, such as cultural centers, mosques. It is recruiting and indoctrinating locals through very aggressive conversion programs. It is working with all sorts of extreme NGOs. It has used Venezuela as a platform to connect with ALBA countries NGO across the continent. So in short, it is trying to use Venezuela and, more broadly, the continent as a forward operating base to expand its influence, push back against the United States influence, and potentially also create operational basis to act against the United States.

Mr. ROONEY. Thank you, sir.

Thank you, chairman.

Mr. COOK. Thank you, sir.

I now recognize Congresswoman Torres from California.

Mrs. TORRES. Thank you, Mr. Chairman. And I believe congratulations are in order. This is your first meeting serving as the chairman of our subcommittee. Let me remind you that you have very big shoes to fill with our former chairman. We went on a trip to South America that I don't think I really understood what we were getting into, and I am so happy that we were able to manage.

Drug trafficking is obviously a very serious problem throughout our hemisphere. And our response to this epidemic has to start not just at home, but we have to look beyond that at cracking down on the illegal flow of narcotics and drugs. And we seem to be losing that battle, at least from the perspective of the Pacific Ocean and how—I don't think that we have worked as closely as we could with our partners in both Central and South America to help them help us intercept the drugs that are coming north.

We also need to work in the region to build up their criminal justice systems and fight corruption. Working to support groups like CICIG innovative approaches which has done so much work in Guatemala, very good work. We also need to work with our partners who seize the drug shipments and utilize tools that we have, sanctioning tools, including the Kingpin Act and the Magnitsky Act are very important tools that we could use.

In Guatemala, we have supported the efforts of CICIG. And the Attorney General, to combat organized crime and corruption, they have made a lot of progress and have put dangerous criminals behind bars, corrupt politicians included.

Now, it appears that CICIG and the Attorney General have become victims of their own success. They have faced threats, smeared campaigns, threw troll banks that have began a campaign effort to discredit their work in attempts to undermine the work that they do.

Mr. Olson, is it true that drug cartels and other criminal organizations commonly finance political campaigns in Central America? And are you aware of any instances where these illicit actors have attempted to directly interfere in elections by supporting disinformation campaigns or troll banks, as I started to call them.

Mr. OLSON. Thank you, Mrs. Torres, Representative Torres. I appreciate your interest and your work on Guatemala and Central America, which is often overlooked as an important part of our region. And in answer to your question, absolutely. You mentioned CICIG. CICIG did a major report on money laundering and attempts of the past President who is currently in prison to use his political party as a money laundering vehicle to run his campaign.

And there has been evidence of other cases in Central America, in Mexico, often at a local level, where criminal organizations, not for ideological reasons, supporting a political party, but simply to gain access and guarantee their own impunity, use the weak campaign finance laws to manipulate and control the process.

So for me, this is a little bit of the original sin for a lot of the people—governments in Latin America where people use weak campaign finance laws to begin the process of corruption that later allows for the burgeoning of criminal organizations and drug trafficking. And there is no question that they use modern communication techniques to influence that process.

Mrs. TORRES. Mr. Semesky, I recently was made aware of a contract, a lobbying contract, that Guatemala officials signed to lobby against CICIG and the Attorney General, to lobby Members of Congress here. Since that contract, I guess, was discovered, it has been terminated.

My office has inquired within our Attorney General's office to investigate the third-party payer, which I believe to be tied to illicit activities.

What are our options there? And I believe I ran out of time. I hope that maybe you can write back and answer to what are some of the options that we can do to approach that.

Mr. SEMESKY. I will do that.

Mrs. TORRES. Thank you.

I yield back, Mr. Chairman.

Mr. COOK. Thank you very much.

I recognize the Congressman from Florida, Chairman Yoho.

Mr. YOHO. Congratulations there, Colonel Cook, on your chairmanship. Good job. I appreciate you all being here. This is such an important hearing. I don't know where to start.

You know, we have seen the war on drugs since the 1990s, if not before, and we have spent trillions of dollars through foreign aid on the war on drugs. But as was mentioned here, the increased growth in Colombia, the increased growth of the poppy fields in Afghanistan, and then I am reading, in Mexico, cultivation of the opium poppy, a primary source of heroin in the United States is also increased to satisfy the increasing demand of the Americans and the rest of the world.

And according to U.S. estimates, Mexico has experienced an increase of more than double of its opium poppy cultivation from 12,000 hectares in 2011 to 28,000 in 2015. 28,000 hectares, if I do my math, it is probably close to 56,000, 60,000 acres in our southern neighbor.

And, you know, I would like to have some of your input. You know, the war on drugs and with the initiatives that we have done have gone after the kingpins, but we have seen the kingpins kind of morph, change the organizations. And one of the questions I want to ask, just get your opinion, if we have a trading partner like Mexico in NAFTA, should we bring that into a trade negotiation and just say, You need to stop it? And I know that is not in the realm of this committee. And if you don't want to weigh in on it, that is okay. If you want to write me a written response, that would be okay.

But I would like to ask you just your opinion, because to do business with countries that are supplying a drug that has virtually no medicinal use and it creates the mayhem we see, what are your thoughts? If you want to start there, Mr. Semesky?

Mr. SEMESKY. Congressman, first of all, let me reiterate that I am not here as a representative of the DEA. I am here as a private citizen. I am retired.

Mr. YOHO. Okay. As a private citizen and probably a parent, maybe?

Mr. SEMESKY. And a parent. And I agree with you completely. It should be part of any negotiations. But just as our demand reduction should be taken into account.

Mr. YOHO. Well, that is something we have to deal with. I mean, we need to deal with that——

Mr. SEMESKY. I first got involved in narcotics investigations with the Organized Crime Drug Enforcement Task Force, or OCDETF, in 1983. And at that point, we were all told, Just put your thumb in the dike. We are going to take care of this on the demand side.

Mr. YOHO. Right. Well, the dike is overflowing.

Mr. SEMESKY. Exactly.

Mr. YOHO. Let me move on to something else, because this is something that—you know, I have been in Congress 5 years now, and I have watched the development of the Iran nuclear deal, and I saw the billions of dollars being taken over there.

Have you seen an increase in Hezbollah and/or Iran in the South American or Central American areas? Anybody want to weigh in on that.

Mr. OTTOLENGHI. I do, sir.

Mr. YOHO. That could be attributed to the increased cash flow.

Mr. OTTOLENGHI. I think that the increased cash flow is helping.

Mr. YOHO. Sure.

Mr. OTTOLENGHI. But it is not the main driver. I think that the reason why you see an increased presence and activity in Latin America in conjunction with organized crime by Hezbollah is driven primarily by the fact that Hezbollah, since 2006, when—you know, it took a severe beating from Israel in the summer war the two sides had with each other, Hezbollah made a decision to shift a significant amount of its revenue sources from organized crime. And in this past decade, it has expanded dramatically to build a

global empire which, according to some sources, at least that I have spoken to, may actually outweigh the contributions that come from Iran. So you have, certainly, an ascendant Iran with a lot more resources supporting Hezbollah, Hezbollah involved in significantly larger activities than it ever was, its involvement in the war in Syria cost an enormous amount of money, and the necessity to build alternative sources to fund that——

Mr. YOHO. All right. Let me move on to something else, and I appreciate your input on that. We talked about how the drug cartels have morphed. What way has the transnational criminal organization adapted to avoid sanctions or minimized the kingpin designation effectiveness?

And has the U.S. sanctions regime related to the king regimen related to kingpin's designation kept pace with the changes in drug trafficking?

And, Mr. Hall, I want to specifically ask you. You mentioned the 50 percent rule. What would you recommend? If you want to start off with those two questions.

Mr. HALL. Thank you.

In terms of the 50 percent rule, I don't—and, again, this is just to clarify when we were talking about this before. I don't have any problem with—and I don't want to limit OFAC's ability to identify sanctioned entities. What I am talking about is putting the burden under strict liability on individual businesses to do that for OFAC. That is what I think is ineffective.

So to answer your question, the 50 percent rule, as it applies to businesses, shouldn't exist. And I also think it also illustrates why there should be a safe harbor that is an escape for strict liability.

Mr. YOHO. Thank you. I am over my time.

Thank you, Mr. Chairman.

Mr. COOK. Thank you, sir.

Our last member is the next manager of the New York Yankees, Representative Espaillat.

Mr. ESPAILLAT. Thank you.

I asked for Girardi to go.

Mr. COOK. I kind of figured that.

No, no. We can't lose you here.

Congressman from New York.

Mr. ESPAILLAT. Chairman, congratulations on your new appointment. And I hope you keep Mr. Sires in check.

Mr. COOK. He is bigger than me. I will do the best I can.

Mr. ESPAILLAT. I look forward to working with both of you as well.

Mr. COOK. Thank you.

Mr. ESPAILLAT. I did enjoy our codel to Europe. I had a good time.

Like so many communities across the country, the district that I represent has seen increases in prescription pain killers, heroin. Particularly East Harlem continues to have a major problem with drug trafficking. And the impact of the Kingpin Act is critical. It touches on my district and my neighborhood as well.

Just recently, the Trump administration declared the opioid crisis a national public health emergency. But there was one tiny major issue with that announcement. It had no funding and no backing aside from the acknowledgement of the epidemic itself. As this relates to Latin America of the tier one kingpin designation, which means they represent the most significant threats and concern with drug trafficking, 65 out of the 110 tier one designations are in the Western Hemisphere. So this committee must and will deal with that particular issue.

To make matters worse, gangs in El Salvador, Honduras, Guatemala, and Nicaragua are profiting from these illicit drugs, and they are taking advantage of poor countries. Yet we saw that, 2 days ago, the Trump administration pulled the TPS for Nicaragua and only briefly extended it for Honduras. I feel that the lack of funding and pulling TPS and this misguided foreign policy direction by the Trump administration confer the cost, instability in the region.

I am also concerned with human trafficking and drug trafficking in the Caribbean. That is why I commissioned a GAO study to analyze the impact of the Caribbean Basin Security Initiative, CBSI, which has been one of the U.S. main vehicles for countering drug trafficking in that region. I think we need to be investing more funding. I look forward to sharing that study with my colleagues and this committee once it comes out.

Mr. Semesky, do you think that the Treasury Department's office of foreign assets control should expand its designation program to target gangs such as MS-13 which operate in El Salvador, Honduras, Nicaragua, Mexico, and the United States? What is the role of the MS-13-type gangs with regards to kingpins and drug dealers in that region? Are they playing a more active role? We know they are very violent. And are they competing for territory? Or what is the status?

Mr. SEMESKY. I am not an expert on the gangs. To the extent of my knowledge, and, again, I am not here representing the DEA, the gangs form alliances. If you take the Sinaloa Cartel as an example, their business model is not to try to overwhelm but it is to partner. So when they partner with gangs in cities like Chicago, cities like New York, it leverages manpower for them. It expands their distribution network, and they are able to control the drugs in an area by using a gang. The gangs can be—to the extent that they can be connected with an already designated cartel, they could be brought under that designation very quickly to the extent that they are designated themselves as kingpins as long as they meet the criteria for the Kingpin Act, yes, they should be designated.

Mr. ESPAILLAT. Anybody else want to weigh in on the role of the gangs in the regions of Central America and——

Mr. OLSON. Well, the work we have done has looked at exactly what you are saying, the role in the region. And primarily, the gangs are focused on territorial control. Controlling neighborhoods, controlling streets and barrios. I was in a community in Honduras in May, a well-known community where six different groups—and people could go by and tell you which street was controlled by which group. Their business model, if you will, in those neighborhoods is primarily extortion, sale and resale of small amounts of marijuana or other kinds of drugs. But their reach and involvement in grand international trafficking of drugs is—I am not saying it is not existent, but it is not the same as when we think of big transnational organized crime groups like, at one point, the Zeta's or Chapo Guzman's group out of Sinaloa. So I think it is important, it behooves of us, I am not saying one is good and the other is bad. It just behooves us to understand fully and carefully what phenomenon we are dealing with and then how to address it, because they each require a response. They just may require different sorts of responses.

Mr. ESPAILLAT. Thank you so much.

Thank you, Mr. Chairman.

Mr. COOK. Thank you, sir.

I believe that is the last of our members here. I just want to thank everybody. I want to thank the speakers here. I think you have given us a lot. I know the staffs are—I think they are going to talk about some of these things where we can—this is not the first hearing. We are going to go down on kingpins, because—particularly with international terrorism and some of these other organizations, it is just too important, too dangerous. And we are probably going to have more on this.

And thank you for taking the time and sharing your expertise with us. It is greatly appreciated.

With that in mind, this meeting is now adjourned.

[Whereupon, at 3:24 p.m., the subcommittee was adjourned.]

APPENDIX

Material Submitted for the Record

SUBCOMMITTEE HEARING NOTICE
COMMITTEE ON FOREIGN AFFAIRS
U.S. HOUSE OF REPRESENTATIVES
WASHINGTON, DC 20515-6128

Subcommittee on the Western Hemisphere
Paul Cook (CA-08), Chairman

November 8, 2017

TO: MEMBERS OF THE COMMITTEE ON FOREIGN AFFAIRS

You are respectfully requested to attend an OPEN hearing of the Committee on Foreign Affairs, to be held by the Subcommittee on the Western Hemisphere in Room 2172 of the Rayburn House Office Building (and available live on the Committee website at http://www.ForeignAffairs.house.gov):

DATE: Wednesday, November 8, 2017

TIME: 2:00 p.m.

SUBJECT: Examining the Effectiveness of the Kingpin Designation Act in the Western Hemisphere

WITNESSES: Mr. Donald C. Semesky Jr.
(Former Chief, Office of Financial Operations, U.S. Drug Enforcement Administration)

Mr. David Hall
Partner
Wiggin and Dana LLP
(Former Prosecutor, U.S. Department of Justice)

Emanuele Ottolenghi, Ph.D.
Senior Fellow
Center on Sanctions and Illicit Finance
Foundation for Defense of Democracies

Mr. Eric L. Olson
Deputy Director
Latin American Program
Woodrow Wilson Center

By Direction of the Chairman

The Committee on Foreign Affairs seeks to make its facilities accessible to persons with disabilities. If you are in need of special accommodations, please call 202/225-5021 at least four business days in advance of the event, whenever practicable. Questions with regard to special accommodations in general (including availability of Committee materials in alternative formats and assistive listening devices) may be directed to the Committee.

COMMITTEE ON FOREIGN AFFAIRS

MINUTES OF SUBCOMMITTEE ON ___________ *Western Hemisphere* ___________ HEARING

Day__ *Wednesday* __Date______ *11/08/17* ____Room______ *2172*______

Starting Time ___ *2:00pm* ___ Ending Time ___ *3:24pm*___

Recesses | *n/a* | (____to ____) (____to ____) (____to ____) (____to ____) (____to ____) (____to ____)

Presiding Member(s)
Chairman Cook

Check all of the following that apply:

Open Session ☑
Executive (closed) Session ☐
Televised ☑

Electronically Recorded (taped) ☑
Stenographic Record ☑

TITLE OF HEARING:

"Examining the Effectiveness of the Kingpin Designation Act in the Western Hemisphere"

SUBCOMMITTEE MEMBERS PRESENT:

Rep. Brooks, Rep. Yoho, Rep. Rooney, Rep. Sires, Rep. Espaillat, Rep. Kelly, Rep. Torres

NON-SUBCOMMITTEE MEMBERS PRESENT: *(Mark with an * if they are not members of full committee.)*

Rep. Donovan

HEARING WITNESSES: Same as meeting notice attached? Yes ☑ No ☐
(If "no", please list below and include title, agency, department, or organization.)

STATEMENTS FOR THE RECORD: *(List any statements submitted for the record.)*

Chairman Cook QFR's

TIME SCHEDULED TO RECONVENE __________
or
TIME ADJOURNED ____ *3:24*____

____
Subcommittee Staff Associate

Donald C. Semesky, Jr.

Questions for the Record

WHEM Subcommittee Hearing: "Examining the Effectiveness of the Kingpin Designation Act in the Western Hemisphere"
November 8, 2017 at 2:00 p.m. in Rayburn Room 2172

QUESTIONS FOR ALL WITNESSES:

1. <u>Value of Multiple Designations.</u> There are several cases where an entity is designated under both Kingpin and terrorist sanctions programs. Is there evidence that a person designated under multiple sanctions programs would receive greater penalties for violations? In your view, which individuals or entities would benefit from being designated under multiple sanctions programs and how? How effective are sanctions when they are cross-designated?
   - <u>Answer:</u> The impact and effectiveness of multiple designations against an individual or legal entity can be many. In my opinion, multiple designations of narco-terrorists and their organizations would derive the most impact for the following reasons.
     i. Depending on the authority under which a particular sanction was based, e.g. International Emergency Economic Powers Act as opposed to the statutory legislation of the Kingpin Act, the ability of the government to bring criminal charges such as money laundering, may differ.
     ii. Different countries follow certain sanctions lists, and not others. Thus, a country may follow a Kingpin Act designation, but not a Foreign Terrorist Organization designation, and vice versa. Multiple designations against an individual or legal entity may be needed to guarantee that sanctioned entities are impacted in foreign jurisdictions.
     iii. Multiple sanctions will also allow for a wider designation of associated entities, many of which provide the funding, access to the financial system, and money laundering services for the Drug Kingpins or Foreign Terrorist Organization. Using only one type of designation may inhibit the reach of the sanctions to a number of these facilitating entities.

2. <u>Kingpin Process.</u> When the U.S. designates an individual or an entity as a Kingpin, that triggers a block of all property and assets of designated entities and those who support them, prohibits U.S. transactions with designated entities, establishes an annual process for sanctioning the most significant foreign narcotics traffickers, increases civil and criminal penalties, and prevents access to drug traffickers' spouses and children to get visas to the U.S. To what extent can designated entities continue to operate outside of the U.S. financial system in informal economies? What can the U.S. and partner nations do to target the informal networks?
   - <u>Answer:</u> Informal financial networks have been around for thousands of years, and always seem to be able to morph and reinvent themselves to answer any government intervention. For the most part, these networks did not originate as criminal financial networks; however, their dearth of recordkeeping, lack of government oversight, and ability to operate almost completely outside of formal financial systems, make them attractive and vulnerable to criminal exploitation. Like the criminal organizations who

exploit them, these informal financial networks depend heavily on communications to conduct their business activities. The ability of U.S. and foreign law enforcement counterparts to intercept communications for violations of money laundering and Bank Secrecy Act (BSA), or similar reporting violations is important in tracking and assigning beneficial ownership to drug proceeds as it changes nature and form during its journey back to its beneficial owner(s). These intercepts are also the only way to document the knowledge and intent of the operators within the informal financial networks, which, in these types of investigations is the most difficult element of the money laundering crime to prove. Legislation, training, and funding are keys to being able to carry out these types of operations. There are also a number of areas that the U.S. and its partners could address that would have even more impact on Kingpins than trying to corral informal value transfer systems.

    i. <u>Address corruption</u>: The number one thing that every Kingpin needs in order to succeed is corruption. Foreign-based Kingpins need corrupt individuals in government and private sectors to carry on their operations. Unfortunately, many times, this corruption is coerced, and not invited. The U.S. needs to work with its foreign partners to come up with strategies and programs to address this problem from a systemic and not an individual case approach.

    ii. <u>Address weak oversight of foreign financial sectors</u>: Most countries have enacted anti-money laundering legislation and suspicious activity reporting. However, these laws and regulations are only as good as the regulatory and enforcement efforts behind them. If the financial institutions think they can operate freely without fear of being discovered and punished, they are more likely to become complicit and/or not address vulnerabilities. An aggravating factor that figures into this equation is the lack of resources and training that government regulatory and enforcement agencies suffer from in most parts of the world. This needs to be addressed as well.

    iii. <u>Address offshore and domestic shell corporations and offshore banking</u>: To start with, Congress needs to pass H.R.3089 - Corporate Transparency Act of 2017, to begin the process of reining in the abuse of US domestic corporate structures, specifically LLCs, both here in the U.S. and abroad, for the purpose of money laundering. Once we have our own house in some semblance of order, we need to aggressively address the abuse of offshore shell corporations and banks. The use of offshore havens to facilitate money laundering through opaque corporate and banking structures are one of the major keys in attacking the wealth of Drug Kingpins as well as the flow of licit and illicit funds that finance and support terrorist and other criminal activity.

    iv. <u>Share information from U.S. regulatory and enforcement activity against informal financial networks with foreign governments</u>: Much of the illicit drug dollars that are laundered by Drug Kingpins is done so through the sale of those drug proceeds on informal black markets, i.e. The Black Market Peso Exchange (BMPE), both in Colombia and Mexico. FinCEN has executed two Geographic Targeting Orders (GTO) in the last several years against the U.S. based businesses (Los Angeles Fashion District and the Miami Trade Zone) that sell goods to Colombian and Mexican importers who buy these drug dollars to pay their trade debts. There is a mechanism for FinCEN to share this information with its foreign financial intelligence unit (FIU) counterparts in Colombia and Mexico through the "Egmont Group" sharing process. Congress should insure that this is being done; so, that those countries can follow up with regulatory enforcement actions against identified importers who are not accurately reporting the value of their imports.

3. <u>Kingpin Effectiveness Disrupting Networks.</u> There are concerns that Kingpin designations are not effective in disrupting the entire transnational criminal networks but instead only achieve results by taking out the leaders, which then create voids that others subsequently fill. Would you agree? In your opinion, how effective have the Kingpin designations programs been in the fight against drug trafficking in the Western Hemisphere?

- <u>Answer</u>: Kingpin designations are not designed to "take out" anyone, in the sense that they lead to incarceration. They are designed to cripple the designee and his/her associated entities economically. There are two ways that Kingpin designations have been successful in impacting entire transnational criminal networks. OFAC has, at times, designated entire transnational criminal networks instead of just the leader(s). This allows any identified assets within U.S. jurisdiction, not just the leader(s), to be frozen. The naming of as many Tier Two, associated entities as possible accomplishes much the same thing. The other way in which Kingpin designations have been successful in impacting an entire transnational criminal network is when the OFAC sanction is done in conjunction with a law enforcement action. This allows for simultaneous arrest of organization members, and also the freezing and seizure of assets. Transnational criminal networks rarely keep their wealth within U.S. jurisdiction; so, impact is usually dependent on the country(ies), in which these transnational criminal networks operate, following the OFAC list. As I mentioned in my written and oral testimony, the OFAC designation has also become an effective law enforcement tool to reach transnational criminal networks that, for one reason or another, are beyond the reach of traditional law enforcement techniques. At times, it is the OFAC designation that brings the cartel or money laundering organization leaders to the table to negotiate their criminal culpability.

QUESTIONS FOR DONALD SEMESKY:

1. <u>State Department Role in Kingpin.</u> The State Department and U.S. embassies play a significant role in ensuring that U.S. foreign policy is not disrupted by Kingpin designations and sanctions programs. How do you see the Treasury Department's Office of Foreign Assets Control's (OFAC) engagement with State and our embassies, especially in sensitive political situations like Venezuela? Is there anything missing that would make this process more effective and that would garner greater joint support from countries where Kingpin designations occur?

   a. OFAC follows a two-stage process in bringing a Kingpin designation. The first is a formal written process during which the interagency, including the State Department, is notified of the intention to designate, and given a chance for input. The second stage involves on-the-ground meetings with affected agencies to set time lines and plan the roll out of the designation. This would include briefings of State Department officials at the headquarters and embassy levels. My experience is that this is typically a seamless exercise. Obviously, the more sensitive the targeted designee, the longer the process may take before the roll out. Again, my experience is that OFAC has always been willing to coordinate and work with agencies and departments whose interests will be affected by the designation.

2. <u>Criminal Group Adaptations</u>. In the 1990s, the U.S. objective was to combat drug traffickers by targeting their illicit wealth. Over the years, these groups have morphed into exploiting corrupt governments and business leaders in the region to wield far-reaching criminal enterprises. Some cartels have reorganized as more horizontal franchises that no longer have kingpin figures at the top. Has the U.S. sanctions regime related to Kingpin designations kept pace with the changes in drug trafficking organizations?

   a. One of the great benefits of having OFAC investigators permanently assigned to DEA Headquarters and Special Operations Division (SOD) offices, as well as the U.S. embassies in Bogota and Mexico City, is that the OFAC investigators have complete access to DEA intelligence and targeting. This enables OFAC to stay abreast of the constant evolution of the drug cartels and other drug trafficking and drug-money laundering organizations that pose the greatest risk to the United States. Two designations that point out OFAC's ability to apply the Kingpin Act to new drug trafficking risks and corruption are the July 29, 2014 designation of members of a synthetic drug trafficking organization led by Chinese national Zhang Lei (a/k/a Eric Chang), and the February 13, 2017 designation of Venezuelan national and Vice President, Tareck Zaidan El Aissami Maddah.

David L. Hall

Questions for the Record
WHEM Subcommittee Hearing: "Examining the Effectiveness of the Kingpin Designation Act in the Western Hemisphere"
November 8, 2017 at 2:00 p.m. in Rayburn Room 2172

Chairman Paul Cook

TO: ALL WITNESSES

1. <u>Value of Multiple Designations.</u> There are several cases where an entity is designated under both Kingpin and terrorist sanctions programs. Is there evidence that a person designated under multiple sanctions programs would receive greater penalties for violations? In your view, which individuals or entities would benefit from being designated under multiple sanctions programs and how? How effective are sanctions when they are cross-designated?

David L. Hall Response:

Thank you, Chairman Cook, for this additional opportunity to share my views with regard to the effectiveness of the Kingpin Designation Act (the "Kingpin Act") and other economic sanctions programs administered by the Department of Treasury, Office of Foreign Assets Control ("OFAC"). As you know from my testimony before the Subcommittee, and my corresponding written statement, my focus is on the effect of sanctions programs on non-criminal U.S. businesses and multi-national businesses operating in the United States. While the primary goal of the Kingpin Act and other sanctions programs is to cripple the financial capabilities of criminal and terrorist organizations, the sanctions themselves are primarily enforced against non-criminal businesses that have inadvertently engaged in prohibited transactions with Specially Designated Nationals and Blocked Persons ("SDNs") – not the SDNs themselves.

For most businesses, the particular sanctions program under which an SDN is identified is not especially relevant – and so it follows that most businesses are not focused on whether an SDN is identified under more than one sanctions program. Therefore, designation under multiple sanctions programs, in and of itself, is not likely to prevent a business from violating the law. While there are some variations among sanctions programs, a U.S. person is generally prohibited from engaging in nearly all transactions with an SDN regardless of the program under which the SDN was designated For a business subject to U.S. jurisdiction, two primary factors will determine the effectiveness of an SDN designation: 1) whether the business conducts third party screening as part of its own internal compliance program; and 2) whether the designated party is accurately identified during third party screening. If a business conducts third party screening and identifies an SDN during its screening, it will likely suspend the transaction regardless of the specific SDN designation of the individual or entity.

2. <u>Kingpin Process.</u> When the U.S. designates an individual or an entity as a Kingpin, that triggers a block of all property and assets of designated entities and those who support them, prohibits

U.S. transactions with designated entities, establishes an annual process for sanctioning the most significant foreign narcotics traffickers, increases civil and criminal penalties, and prevents access to drug traffickers' spouses and children to get visas to the U.S. To what extent can designated entities continue to operate outside of the U.S. financial system in informal economies? What can the U.S. and partner nations to do target the informal networks?

David L. Hall Response:

In practice, the effect of economic sanctions designations on commerce is determined by the risk appetite of individual businesses – and businesses subject to U.S. jurisdiction vary significantly in their risk appetites. As a result, not only do SDNs continue to have access to "informal economies" located outside the United States, but they also have access to U.S. financial systems to the extent they are able to mask their true identities. They can do this by many means including establishing shell-companies that have not yet been identified as designated entities, dealing in cash transactions with smaller U.S. businesses, and utilizing nominees in banking transactions.

In some cases, U.S. businesses manage risk by taking prophylactic "de-risking" measures. In these cases, the business decides that the high cost of compliance and the potential for significant civil monetary penalties is untenable, and stops doing business in high risk regions and high risk business sectors categorically. In a 2016 article, Reuters provided an example of how de-risking can have unintended consequences, particularly in small countries like Belize.[1] The ultimate effect on affected nations is difficult to predict. On the one hand, de-risking could cause them to strengthen their own anti-money laundering compliance regimes. On the other hand, the loss of access to the U.S. financial system could drive them out of the U.S. sphere of influence altogether, leading to increased business dealings with sanctioned entities. All of this is the result of OFAC's strict liability standard and the severe potential penalties, which combine to impose enormous risk on businesses, including banks. The multi-million dollar penalties imposed against BNP Paribas SA[2] and HSBC Holdings[3] illustrate the high cost of non-compliance.

3. <u>Kingpin Effectiveness Disrupting Networks.</u> There are concerns that Kingpin designations are not effective in disrupting the entire transnational criminal networks but instead only achieve results by taking out the leaders, which then create voids that others subsequently fill. Would you agree? In your opinion, how effective have the Kingpin designations programs been in the fight against drug trafficking in the Western Hemisphere?

---

[1] Yeganeh Torbati, <u>Caribbean countries caught in crossfire of U.S. crackdown on illicit money flow</u>, Reuters (July 12, 2016, 5:00 PM), https://www.reuters.com/investigates/special-report/usa-banking-caribbean/#video-caribbean.

[2] In a settlement agreement with OFAC in 2014, BNP Paribas SA agreed to pay a civil penalty of $963,619,900 for 3,897 apparent violations of the Sudanese Sanctions Regulations, the Iranian Transactions and Sanctions Regulations, the Cuban Assets Control Regulations, and the Burmese Sanctions Regulations. *See* OFAC Web Notice of Enforcement Information for June 30, 2014, available at https://www.treasury.gov/resource-center/sanctions/CivPen/Documents/20140630_bnp.pdf.

[3] In a settlement agreement with OFAC in 2012, HSBC Holdings plc agreed to pay a civil penalty of $375,000,000 for apparent violations of the Iran Transactions Regulations, the Burmese Sanctions Regulations, the Sudanese Sanctions Regulations, the Cuban Assets Control Regulations, and the Libyan Sanctions Regulations. *See* OFAC Web Notice of Enforcement Information for December 11, 2012, available at https://www.treasury.gov/resource-center/sanctions/CivPen/Documents/121211_HSBC_posting.pdf.

David L. Hall Response:

I cannot speak directly to the effectiveness of the Kingpin designations in disrupting transnational criminal networks. However, I do recommend that Congress request a comprehensive review by the United States Government Accountability Office of the effectiveness of the Specially Designated Nationals and Blocked Persons designations overall. As I understand from testimony at the Subcommittee hearing, no such study has been conducted. Given the significant cost imposed on U.S. businesses by sanctions programs, it seems advisable to undertake an evaluation of the benefits of such programs.

TO: MR. HALL

1. <u>Kingpin Effect of Sanctions on Private Sector.</u> On August 13, 2014, the Treasury Department issued revised guidance on the so-called "50% rule," which clarifies that assets of an entity that is 50% or more owned, directly or indirectly, by a person, or persons in aggregate, on the Specially Designated Nationals (SDN) List are also blocked, even if that entity is not listed itself. Can you describe how small and medium size businesses are impacted by the enforcement of these sanctions programs compared to large corporations and financial institutions? How does this impact banks in the Caribbean, which are often small?

David L. Hall Response:

To date, only one major enforcement action has identified violations of the "50 Percent Rule."[4] Nevertheless, the existence of the rule itself places a substantial compliance burden on companies – especially those with significant international business or operating in higher risk industries. The increased compliance burden is not justified by any increase in the effectiveness of the underlying sanctions program. This is because the 50 Percent Rule puts businesses in the position of acting as a stop-gap to identify entities owned by SDNs that the government has not been able to identify. Even companies with robust compliance programs that take into account the ownership structure of potential customers and vendors will likely fail at helping the government achieve this goal for the following reasons.

- **First**, businesses, especially small- to medium-sized businesses, have limited resources available for identifying ownership information. Private companies are not required to disclose ownership percentages to third parties or even to name individual owners on state incorporation documents. Determining ownership information for international companies is especially difficult when little public information is available or is only available in a

---

[4] In February 2016, OFAC entered into a settlement agreement with UK bank Barclays Bank Plc for apparent violations of the Zimbabwe Sanctions Regulations. According to the settlement agreement, Barclays allegedly processed 159 U.S. dollar transactions totaling $3,375,617 on behalf of customers that were more than 50 percent owned by Industrial Development Corporation of Zimbabwe, an SDN. *See* Tahlia Townsend, Dan Goren & Matthew Nettleton, *OFAC Fines Foreign Bank for Violating 50 Percent Rule*, Wiggin and Dana, Advisory (Feb. 9, 2016), http://www.wiggin.com/16374.

foreign language. In some cases, foreign business partners are not permitted by foreign law to provide such information.

- **Second**, businesses conducting ownership due diligence do not typically share the results of their diligence with other businesses or with the government. While some businesses, such as banks, do file Suspicious Activity Reports with the government, these disclosures are not public documents. And in most cases, the internal compliance determinations of businesses are not reported to the government. Thus, when a business does identify an entity that is fifty percent owned by an SDN, in most cases, no one else learns about it.

- **Finally**, transaction-based due diligence is expensive. Most companies – particularly small businesses – do not conduct this level of diligence. Those that do usually rely on high level searches of free or low-cost databases – that are not always current or accurate. The cost of using an outside investigative service or employees to conduct detailed searches of public databases is simply cost prohibitive for many businesses.

If businesses are not successfully identifying upstream ownership, either because they are not conducting due diligence or because that diligence is not effective, the 50 Percent Rule becomes meaningless as a deterrent.

OFAC sanctions are not surgical. Particularly blunt is the 50 Percent Rule, which does not even identify the target of sanctions. Leaving that to U.S. businesses is inherently ineffective. For this reason, the 50 Percent Rule should be eliminated.

TO: MR. SEMESKY

1. State Department Role in Kingpin. The State Department and U.S. embassies play a significant role in ensuring that U.S. foreign policy is not disrupted by Kingpin designations and sanctions programs. How do you see the Treasury Department's Office of Foreign Assets Control's (OFAC) engagement with State and our embassies, especially in sensitive political situations like Venezuela? Is there anything missing that would make this process more effective and that would garner greater joint support from countries where Kingpin designations occur?

2. Criminal Group Adaptations. In the 1990s, the U.S. objective was to combat drug traffickers by targeting their illicit wealth. Over the years, these groups have morphed into exploiting corrupt governments and business leaders in the region to wield far-reaching criminal enterprises. Some cartels have reorganized as more horizontal franchises that no longer have kingpin figures at the top. Has the U.S. sanctions regime related to Kingpin designations kept pace with the changes in drug trafficking organizations?

Emanuele Ottolenghi

Questions for the Record
WHEM Subcommittee Hearing: "Examining the Effectiveness of the Kingpin Designation Act in the Western Hemisphere"
November 8, 2017 at 2:00 p.m. in Rayburn Room 2172

Chairman Paul Cook

TO: ALL WITNESSES

1. <u>Value of Multiple Designations.</u> There are several cases where an entity is designated under both Kingpin and terrorist sanctions programs. Is there evidence that a person designated under multiple sanctions programs would receive greater penalties for violations? In your view, which individuals or entities would benefit from being designated under multiple sanctions programs and how? How effective are sanctions when they are cross-designated?

   EMANUELE OTTOLENGHI: There is value in double designations for mainly two reasons. A Kingpin designation extends penalties to spouses and children. Someone currently designated for terrorism, such as is the case with Latin America based Hezbollah operatives, can easily transfer the day to day handling of financial transactions and nominal ownership of their businesses to their family members. A Kingpin designation would further limit their room for maneuver. Also, U.S. partners may not always be willing to act on terrorism designations. A Kingpin designation against U.S. designated terrorists would provide the legal basis for allied countries to act against U.S. designated terrorists, albeit on criminal grounds.

   In terms of which individuals or entities would be most suitable for multiple designations, I strongly recommend using multiple sanctions instruments against Hezbollah and Iran's Islamic Revolutionary Guards Corps, or IRGC. As indicated in my written testimony, Hezbollah draws a significant part of its operating budget from its participation in illicit activities that include drug trafficking. A Kingpin designation for Hezbollah and its leadership would send a powerful message to the world that Hezbollah is a criminal syndicate as well as a Global Terrorist Organization.

   As for the IRGC, the process should be similar. Treasury targeted Gholamreza Baghbani, a senior IRGC's Quds Force general, in 2012, for his role coordinating transfers of opium from Afghanistan through Iran. Linking the IRGC and senior members in its command structure to the drug trade through Kingpin designations highlights the proximity between the Iranian regime and its revolutionary institutions on the one hand, and international drug trafficking networks on the other. It creates a public stigma and helps the United States make a strong case about sanctioning the IRGC with allies who are reluctant to treat them as a terror organization.

2. <u>Kingpin Process.</u> When the U.S. designates an individual or an entity as a Kingpin, that triggers a block of all property and assets of designated entities and those who support them, prohibits U.S. transactions with designated entities, establishes an annual process for sanctioning the most significant foreign narcotics traffickers, increases civil and criminal penalties, and

prevents access to drug traffickers' spouses and children to get visas to the U.S. To what extent can designated entities continue to operate outside of the U.S. financial system in informal economies? What can the U.S. and partner nations to do target the informal networks?

EMANUELE OTTOLENGHI: Designated entities can continue to operate, albeit at a significant premium cost and with considerable additional impediments, outside of the U.S. financial system. Informal economies can certainly make that task easier. That's why sanctions must be followed by U.S. diplomatic efforts with allies to persuade them to enforce them. They must be coupled with prosecutions. And where possible, they must be expanded to target local facilitators and enablers.

Kingpin designated entities tend to be involved in the movement of large sums of money due to the nature of their illicit trade. However circuitous and convoluted their operations may be, they eventually require access to the global financial system in order to launder drug proceeds. A sustained effort to target those facilitators and enablers around Kingpin designated entities would no doubt enhance the effectiveness of this tool. The possible punishment of financial institutions in the process, through either sanctions, Patriot Act 311 designations, or civil forfeiture actions would also create strong incentives for allied countries to act against designated entities operating in their own jurisdiction.

3. Kingpin Effectiveness Disrupting Networks. There are concerns that Kingpin designations are not effective in disrupting the entire transnational criminal networks but instead only achieve results by taking out the leaders, which then create voids that others subsequently fill. Would you agree? In your opinion, how effective have the Kingpin designations programs been in the fight against drug trafficking in the Western Hemisphere?

EMANUELE OTTOLENGHI: TO answer this question I would like to draw your attention to the Kingpin designation of the Waked money laundering organization announced by Treasury in May 2016. Since the designation happened, the U.S. has used the Kingpin Act to ensure that targeted entities would divest themselves of their assets. This has been the case already with several financial institutions that the Waked MLO controlled in Panama. U.S. pressure combined with cooperation with local authorities led to these assets being removed from the control of targeted entities. This is a clear example of how the threat of serious economic consequences spurs government to government cooperation and leads to positive results. Also, the same designation shows that while the Kingpin Act targets entities at the top of the pyramid, there is significant latitude to expand its impact. In the case of the Waked MLO, Treasury was able to target dozens of companies and individuals. Treasury has the power to de-designate but also to add new entities to the same designation if follow-ups uncovered new evidence. In other words, the legislation is flexible enough. It leaves enough leeway to the executive to go after more than those who sit at the top of a criminal structure.

TO: MR. HALL

1. Kingpin Effect of Sanctions on Private Sector. On August 13, 2014, the Treasury Department issued revised guidance on the so-called "50% rule," which clarifies that assets of an entity that is 50% or more owned, directly or indirectly, by a person, or persons in aggregate, on the

Specially Designated Nationals (SDN) List are also blocked, even if that entity is not listed itself. Can you describe how small and medium size businesses are impacted by the enforcement of these sanctions programs compared to large corporations and financial institutions? How does this impact banks in the Caribbean, which are often small?

TO: MR. SEMESKY

1. <u>State Department Role in Kingpin.</u> The State Department and U.S. embassies play a significant role in ensuring that U.S. foreign policy is not disrupted by Kingpin designations and sanctions programs. How do you see the Treasury Department's Office of Foreign Assets Control's (OFAC) engagement with State and our embassies, especially in sensitive political situations like Venezuela? Is there anything missing that would make this process more effective and that would garner greater joint support from countries where Kingpin designations occur?

2. <u>Criminal Group Adaptations</u>. In the 1990s, the U.S. objective was to combat drug traffickers by targeting their illicit wealth. Over the years, these groups have morphed into exploiting corrupt governments and business leaders in the region to wield far-reaching criminal enterprises. Some cartels have reorganized as more horizontal franchises that no longer have kingpin figures at the top. Has the U.S. sanctions regime related to Kingpin designations kept pace with the changes in drug trafficking organizations?

Eric Olson

Questions for the Record

WHEM Subcommittee Hearing: "Examining the Effectiveness of the Kingpin Designation Act in the Western Hemisphere"
November 8, 2017 at 2:00 p.m. in Rayburn Room 2172

Chairman Paul Cook

TO: ALL WITNESSES

1. Value of Multiple Designations. There are several cases where an entity is designated under both Kingpin and terrorist sanctions programs. Is there evidence that a person designated under multiple sanctions programs would receive greater penalties for violations? In your view, which individuals or entities would benefit from being designated under multiple sanctions programs and how? How effective are sanctions when they are cross-designated?

   OLSON: I haven't studied the issue of cross designation so do not have an informed opinion on this issue. As I said at the Hearing and in written testimony, it's time to request a systematic review of these sanction programs to ensure that they are effective.

2. Kingpin Process. When the U.S. designates an individual or an entity as a Kingpin, that triggers a block of all property and assets of designated entities and those who support them, prohibits U.S. transactions with designated entities, establishes an annual process for sanctioning the most significant foreign narcotics traffickers, increases civil and criminal penalties, and prevents access to drug traffickers' spouses and children to get visas to the U.S. To what extent can designated entities continue to operate outside of the U.S. financial system in informal economies? What can the U.S. and partner nations to do target the informal networks?

   OLSON: Sanctions undoubtedly make it harder for the designated person to continue his/her illegal activities but a Kingpin designation does not make this impossible either. The effectiveness of the designation also has to do with the strength of the regulatory agencies and rule of law in the country where the sanctioned person lives or operates. For example, "El Chapo" Guzman was designated under the Kingpin Act in June 2001 but continued operating until his third and final arrest in Mexico in January 2016 and subsequent extradition to the U.S. a year later. Compared to other countries in Central America, Mexico has much greater regulatory capacity and works collaboratively with the U.S.

   The problems become even more pronounced in countries with very weak regulatory frameworks, such as Honduras, and nearly impossible to control in countries where institutionality is almost entirely broken such as Venezuela. In the case of Venezuela government needs to interact with the international financial system because of its petroleum business, so a designation can complicate the life of individuals or entities that need to operation internationally. But this is not enough when the rule of law is non-existent, and where independent regulators, prosecutors, or courts do not exist. This is why simply relying on sanction regimes like the Kingpin Act is insufficient and must be complemented with efforts to strengthen the regulatory capacity in countries where there are sanctioned individuals and entities.

3. <u>Kingpin Effectiveness Disrupting Networks.</u> There are concerns that Kingpin designations are not effective in disrupting the entire transnational criminal networks but instead only achieve results by taking out the leaders, which then create voids that others subsequently fill. Would you agree? In your opinion, how effective have the Kingpin designations programs been in the fight against drug trafficking in the Western Hemisphere?

   OLSON: I agree that Kingpin designations only achieve partial results. This is not to say they have no value. The Act is one tool in the toolbox. Designations can make it more difficult for a criminal to benefit from their illicit business, but they can and do find ways around this. Even if a designation leads to the arrest of an individual, or the shuttering of their business, as in the Rosenthal/Banco Continental case in Honduras I cited in my testimony, the effects are temporary. There isn't much evidence that overall drug trafficking (cocaine in particular) has fallen as a result. Drug trafficking is a business based on supply and demand. To think of it solely as dependent on specific criminal actors, is to miss the underlying factors that drive the business. I believe our main challenge is to think about how to more effectively reduce demand and how to more effectively raise the cost of doing business. The Kingpin Act has been one tool in this process but we cannot assume it will solve the problem.

TO: MR. HALL

1. <u>Kingpin Effect of Sanctions on Private Sector.</u> On August 13, 2014, the Treasury Department issued revised guidance on the so-called "50% rule," which clarifies that assets of an entity that is 50% or more owned, directly or indirectly, by a person, or persons in aggregate, on the Specially Designated Nationals (SDN) List are also blocked, even if that entity is not listed itself. Can you describe how small and medium size businesses are impacted by the enforcement of these sanctions programs compared to large corporations and financial institutions? How does this impact banks in the Caribbean, which are often small?

TO: MR. SEMESKY

1. <u>State Department Role in Kingpin.</u> The State Department and U.S. embassies play a significant role in ensuring that U.S. foreign policy is not disrupted by Kingpin designations and sanctions programs. How do you see the Treasury Department's Office of Foreign Assets Control's (OFAC) engagement with State and our embassies, especially in sensitive political situations like Venezuela? Is there anything missing that would make this process more effective and that would garner greater joint support from countries where Kingpin designations occur?

2. <u>Criminal Group Adaptations</u>. In the 1990s, the U.S. objective was to combat drug traffickers by targeting their illicit wealth. Over the years, these groups have morphed into exploiting corrupt governments and business leaders in the region to wield far-reaching criminal enterprises. Some cartels have reorganized as more horizontal franchises that no longer have kingpin figures at the top. Has the U.S. sanctions regime related to Kingpin designations kept pace with the changes in drug trafficking organizations?

www.ingramcontent.com/pod-product-compliance
Lightning Source LLC
Chambersburg PA
CBHW081315250726
48662CB00008B/2583